The Snow Lotus

ALSO BY PETER M. LESCHAK

Seeing the Raven
Letters from Side Lake
The Bear Guardian
Bumming with the Furies
Hellroaring

The University of Minnesota Press gratefully acknowledges assistance provided for the publication of this volume by the John K. and Elsie Lampert Fesler Fund.

The Snow Lotus

Exploring the Eternal Moment

Peter M. Leschak

 University of Minnesota Press

Minneapolis

London

Portions of this book, in altered form, were first published in *The Brainerd Daily Dispatch, Mpls.-St. Paul Magazine, The Minnesota Volunteer, Lynx Eye*, and *The Window*.

Published by the University of Minnesota Press
111 Third Avenue South, Suite 290
Minneapolis, MN 55401-2520

Book design by Will Powers
Typesetting by Stanton Publication Services, Inc., St. Paul
Printed in the United States of America on acid-free paper

Library of Congress Cataloging-in-Publication Data

Leschak, Peter M., 1951–
    The snow lotus : exploring the eternal moment /
Peter M. Leschak.
        p.   cm.
    ISBN 0-8166-2820-3 (hc)
    1. Minnesota—Description and travel.   2. Natural history—
Minnesota.   3. Leschak, Peter M., 1951–   .   4. Minnesota—
Social life and customs.   I. Title.
F610.L496   1996
917.76—dc20   95-52674

For Pam,
the face in the mirror pond

and for Catherine and Chris,
who love the sky

Whatever lives in time exists in the present and progresses from the past to the future, and there is nothing set in time which can embrace simultaneously the whole extent of its life: it is in the position of not yet possessing tomorrow when it has already lost yesterday. In this life of today you do not live more fully than in that fleeting and transitory moment.

BOETHIUS, The Consolation of Philosophy

Yesterday is ashes, tomorrow is wood, only today does the fire burn brightly.

NATIVE AMERICAN PROVERB

Contents

Acknowledgments

Thanks to Todd Orjala for helping to shape the manuscript, and to Kristine Vesley for helping with the fine-tuning.

And thanks to Hal Rudstrom for being calm and cool when it was needed, and to Mark Adams for guiding me through a memorable cut.

The Snow Lotus

⑤ Deer Beds:
A Prologue

The telephone jangled at 3:32 A.M. After thirteen years as a firefighter—being randomly paged at any and all hours—my conditioned response to such a nighttime call is amusing. I truly cannot move as fast when awake and in daylight.

By the end of the first ring the quilt was off and my feet thumped the floor. I was staring at the digital clock on the dresser: 3–3–2. By the end of the second ring I had covered half the distance to the office phone, in darkness. I vaguely recall butting an obstacle, perhaps the library doorjamb. I clawed at a light switch on the way through, but missed. By the end of the third ring I clutched the receiver in my hand.

"Yeah?" A civil greeting was beyond me.

I was angry and scared. Who in the hell calls at 3:30 in the morning? During the long seconds it took to reach the

1

phone, I imagined two possibilities. Either it was some drunk dialing a wrong number, or a tragedy had befallen a person close to us; someone was in the hospital or the morgue. Fear outweighed anger. My pulse rate was up, and the rings had struck like a trio of rabbit punches to the back of the neck. It hurts to be torn from sound sleep, to be that startled in the dead of night and bang your head against a doorjamb in a semistuporous rush to hear evil news; or, maybe no news—just that damned drunk.

"Yeah?"

There was hollow silence at the other end of the line, and I filled it with additional dread. Was this person struggling to find the right words—any words—to convey the unglad tidings?

Then: "Pete! How are you? This is Cameron."

I finally focused on the din of barroom carousing in the background, and this was no wrong number. I correctly guessed the origin of the call immediately—the beat-up pay phone behind the jukebox at The Triangle Tavern in Grangeville, Idaho. Of all the grand saloons I've patronized west of the Mississippi, it's the most esteemed. Over the course of three summers, while snared in its congenial embrace, I seized a lot of moments—from raucous to reverent. But not at three-stinking-thirty A.M.!

And Cameron? A smokejumper I hadn't seen for two years. We worked wildfire together out of the Forest Service's Grangeville Air Center in '91 and '92, and had also regularly hashed over philosophical and political questions while quaffing Betty's cheap tap beer in the soothing dimness of The Triangle. Cameron is a perspicacious, twenty-something fire grunt/intellectual, and the generational difference spiced our debates.

Realizing that I might be irritated before I was thrilled, Cameron quickly revealed the impetus for his graveyard-shift call. That evening, he told me, a memorial service had been conducted for our colleagues killed in the line of duty during the wild Western fire season of 1994. Two dozen had died—smokejumpers, helitack personnel, pilots, a dozer operator, half of a hotshot crew. It had been a particularly grim year. I was personally acquainted with one of the dead; Cameron had known more. The ceremony, he said, "was a tearjerker," and The Triangle became a postmemorial refuge for many of the firefighters. Naturally, "war stories" —"a hundred of 'em" as Cameron said—soon salted the hubbub and my name came up. He felt compelled to call.

I couldn't be angry, of course. Sure, Cameron was under the maudlin spell of reminiscence and alcohol, but it required genuine effort to track down our number and dial. It would have been much easier to raise a sloshing toast to my memory and call it good enough.

We spoke for a few minutes, trying to catch up, but Cameron was hampered by noise and beer, and I never did attain normal alertness. He kept apologizing for the lateness of the hour, and to say we had a conversation would be stretching it. But sometimes it truly is the thought that counts, and when I hung up I was stirred by the luster of comradeship. The sinewy fetters of time and distance were temporarily loosened by the warmth of touching and being touched, even via telephone at 3:32 A.M.

Later that morning, after scant, fitful sleep, and too much coffee, I hefted my chain saw and slipped into the woods to buck some birch firewood. On approaching the trees I intended to fell, I noticed an oval of flattened grass and ferns. A deer bed. About ten feet farther on there was another, then two more, all arranged in an arc near the birch coppice. They appeared fresh; the grass had not yet rebounded.

On impulse, I knelt beside the first one and placed my palm in the center. I was surprised to feel it was still warm. Doubting this discovery, I laid my other hand on the ground outside the bed. It was noticeably cooler. Apparently, I had just missed these deer, probably spooked them off the beds myself. I kept a hand on the bed for several seconds, absorbing the latent heat, vicariously caressing a deer.

.   .   .   .

I thought of Cameron's phone call. The warmth of our transitory connection was like these perishable imprints of slumbering whitetails. Even as I knelt there, they cooled; in a few days they'd be invisible, the vegetation lifted back in place. We yearn to keep our friends, cherish them, perhaps even cling to them, but all too often the best we can do is brush as they pass—lingering over the temporary warmth. There are not enough days and nights, not enough time for hands to clasp.

"What is life?" asked Crowfoot, a Blackfoot orator. "It is the flash of a firefly in the night. It is the breath of a buffalo in the wintertime. It is the little shadow which runs across the grass and loses itself in the sunset."

These are credited as his last words, and how magnificent to be eloquent at the outer rim of life. But within these flashes, breaths, and shadows, there *is* a path to eternity. I think we all know the way. It is often thorny and steep, but the passage is in plain view. I see it now as I write. . . . Join me in a journey.

⑤ The Snow Lotus

.
.
.
.
.
.
.
.
.
.

*. . . its aim is always and consistently
to be that of which it speaks.*
Thomas Mann

It's a singular season, ripe with old scat, and The Reverend
is attentive. The only time he'll allow me to surge past him
on skis is when he pauses to vigorously sniff at the winter's
accumulation of wolf droppings. I'm pleasantly surprised at
how many there are. It's March 21st, and we have heard the
local pack singing only four times since early November,
but the trail is peppered with dark, furry stools.

Businesslike, but rushed—for I quickly glide ahead—
Rev sprinkles his scent on each collage before sprinting
up and blowing by me to compulsively regain the lead.

"It's your cousins!" I yell at his rump. But he's intent on this bonanza of spoor and pays no heed. In the house he studies my subtlest nuance of expression and mood, perking his ears at the sound of my voice. In the woods he's fixated on the odor of his cousins and the joy of running. I'm just the big dog he lopes with.

It's a day after the vernal equinox, officially spring, and the snow is crusted and durable. I can ski anywhere—cutting through bogs, darting between black spruce and tamaracks, or abandoning the trail on a sudden whim to skate across a beaver pond—and over "deer berry" depressions. More scat. The clusters of dark brown deer pellets have been absorbing the increasingly potent rays of the late-winter sun, and thus heated, have sunk below the surface of the snow to form circular pockets, like nests of tiny eggs. These are seeds of winter's dissolution; bare ground or open water will appear beneath these droppings soon.

Actually, several days of warm, sunny weather have created snowfree patches on the trail and around the base of nearly every tree. At one point a pair of ruffed grouse startle us as they burst into the air from sanctuary under a balsam fir. They have been nestled in a swath of sun-dappled dry grass and clover. The Rev briefly charges off in the direction of their flight. He hasn't had the chance to jump a grouse since last autumn's hunting season.

There are a few puffs of cumulus cloud overhead—long absent from the wintry atmosphere—and the morning sky seems particularly bright and blue. If I were looking only upward it would be easy to imagine we were already blessed by May or July. But this time of year the ground is far more interesting. The snowpack is hard enough to support me, but a recent veneer faithfully preserves everyone else's tracks.

I note where a squirrel leaped off the lower branches of a white spruce, punching a small crater in the snow; its subsequent footprints are low-impact impressions, so fine that I can discern the mark of each toe.

I see the chickenlike talon tracks of a grouse, one step set precisely in front of the other, and touching—as if the prints were rolled off a strip of adhesive and stretched out in the snow.

The crust is armored to withstand even the the sharp hooves of deer, and I ski over a chopped-up portion of trail where at least two whitetails danced a stutter step without breaking through, then leaped off into the alder brush. The prints are fresh. Perhaps they heard me and Rev approaching. We're not renowned for stealth—especially with skis buffing flinty snow.

I see the tracks of hare, foxes, voles, and of course wolves, plus the sheerest gravure of all—the tandem sweep of raven wings, like arcing brush strokes on a crystalline canvas. They barely show up on this snowpack, ephemeral feather swipes that strikingly evoke the grace of liftoff. I recall the first time I noticed such marks in the snow. For a moment I was baffled, couldn't make sense of the weird artistry. Then I laughed with the sudden delight of recognition. Wing tracks!—the traceless spoor of flight made visible.

Not far from the splatter of hoofprints I double-pole down a short hill, digging in for speed, forcing The Rev to kick into high gear. I'm right on his tail, chanting "Hup! Hup! Hup!" just to keep him wired and provoke a race. He beats me to the bottom, and without breaking stride crests the top of a beaver dam that merges with the base of the slope. I intend to traverse the dam also, but there's a bare patch of grass and cattails directly ahead. It appears narrow enough to "jump"—that is, the tips of my skis will contact the snow on the other side before the ends of the skis leave the snow in the rear, thus bridging the naked ground. It'll slow me, but that should be all.

Wrong. In my exuberance I've misjudged the width by at least a foot. Both skis skid full-length into dry grass and stop dead. I attain liftoff, literally flying forward in a near-perfect somersault. Half by accident I manage a graceless but effective tuck, slamming into the snow on my left shoulder and

. . . .

arm instead of my face. (That would have fashioned an interesting impression.) Except for a bruised palm that strikes a rock or stick beneath the shattered crust, I'm unhurt. I'm also relieved no skis are broken.

I lie there a moment, stunned by the instantaneous transformation from swooping glide to grounded, tangled skis. The Reverend has halted, gazing back over his haunch, expressionless. How polite. He waits until I struggle upright, then trots off across the dam, nose to the trail.

I stand for a spell, leaning forward on my poles. I do that a lot. It's akin to the lotus position, a stimulus to meditation.

There's a black-capped chickadee flitting about the branches of a nearby aspen, and I muse on the events of the previous day. Not only did astronomical spring arrive—at 2:30 P.M.—but around noon a slate-colored junco landed on the mound of sunflower seeds beneath the feeders. I whooped and called Pam to the window. The vernal equinox is usually meaningless in this part of the world, at least as far as weather is concerned. Indeed, it was snowing at 2:30. But a junco is a genuine harbinger. The previous November 11th was the last day we'd seen one at the feeder—128 days before, an accurate measure for the span of hard winter.

It had been a long frigid season, memorable for a near-record cold snap. In mid-January I was interviewed by the BBC out of London, urged to spin Klondike-esque tales for those who could scarcely imagine the Arctic tenor of our subzero afternoon highs. It was a protracted siege even for us.

But I had recently told a friend that despite the newsworthy cold, I would recall this season as "the winter I read *The Magic Mountain*." I started Thomas Mann's massive novel at the turn of the year, and worked at it for nearly two months. It's not light reading, and frankly tough going in parts, but also an adventure. At the climax—an intellectual and emotional tour de force—the hero, Hans Castorp, seemed as real (or more so) than many people I know in the flesh. Joseph Campbell, in his own masterpiece, *Creative Mythology*, referred often to *The Magic Mountain*, calling it

. . . .

"a symphony" and asserting "the novel is readily available and certainly to be read, one of the five or six greatest of the century." I took it to heart and ordered a copy (it wasn't readily available in northern Minnesota).

I quickly realized that deep winter is the appropriate bimester to join Hans Castorp on his quest. In one of the most vibrant scenes, Castorp is lost on skis in a blizzard. Skiing, a virgin undertaking for him, had been a revelation, and it seems fitting that amid the fear and confusion of being astray in the mountains, he experiences a dream/hallucination that is pivotal to his story—and to humanity's. I was stunned. (I will not detract from your potential awe by revealing the vision here.) And how excellent that Castorp was on skis!

Campbell also stated that *The Magic Mountain* "is much too rich in life and in closely interwoven ideas to be summarized, or even adequately suggested." However, in musing on Castorp's "vision ski," I was reminded of an aphorism by Wittgenstein: "If we take eternity to mean not infinite temporal duration, but timelessness, then eternal life belongs to those who live in the present."

To those, in other words, who pay attention and are engaged with the world; to the keen observers, the hunters of perceptions. To, I suppose, The Reverend intently sniffing at spoor—and to anyone immersed in *The Magic Mountain*, or its like.

As I push off my poles and follow Rev across the beaver dam, it's clear to me that reading is as real as wolf shit. And it's also evident that each time my ski poles pierce the snow I am stabbing at eternity.

.   .   .   .

Snow White
and the Timberwolf

Patience, and shuffle the cards.
CERVANTES, Don Quixote

If you slice an apple in half crosswise, the bisected seed pod
will appear as a near-perfect five-pointed star, which is, traditionally, a symbol of immortality. In the proper setting—
say, a party where wine has nudged the perceptions of the
resident metaphysicians (and aren't we all?)—a demonstration can be dramatic, especially when wielding a big knife.

In Celtic myth, apples were representative of immortality
via wisdom, so it's not surprising that although the Book of
Genesis doesn't specify which fruit the Serpent convinced
Eve and Adam to consume illicitly, subsequent legend insisted it was an apple. And a pentacle—a five-pointed star—

represents Satan because he was Lucifer, the morning star, and Satan was also the Serpent. And when Snow White's jealous stepmother attempts to murder the beautiful princess she employs what? A poisoned apple. And though Snow White was laid in a glass coffin, she was awakened by the kiss of the prince, so we discover she was immortal, and the poison could not overcome the inherent nature of the apple with its five-pointed star. And so on. We can weave symbol, legend, and fact ad infinitum, because at one point or another everything's connected in a vast network of meaning.

At 3:45 P.M. on April Fool's Day, 1994, just after reading an article about the eventual collapse of the sun and inevitable demise of the earth—our living planet is not immortal—The Reverend and I walked down to the frozen shore of Secret Lake. As we stood on the ice—24 inches thick—I recalled from the article that the sun's luminosity is expected to increase by ten percent over the next 1.1 billion years. That will trigger a runaway greenhouse effect on earth, boiling off the oceans and thus terminating life on the globe as we know it. There's irony in that concept when you're treading on two feet of April ice.

I sat on the edge of the dock, its cedar planks recently emerged from the snow drifts that concealed them since November. I was reveling in the first sixty-degree day of the year, and though the sky was low and hibernal gray, a cordial southwesterly breeze smelled like sunshine. An hour before, I'd actually seen a butterfly. Though the ice sheet could still support the weight of a large truck, I guessed it would be gone in two weeks. Open water is seldom far behind the first butterfly.

I gazed down the shoreline to my left, curious about the riot of ravens. That's what had drawn me to the lake. From the house I'd heard the loud cries and sqawking of several ravens. I now counted about twenty. Most were orbiting a finger of bog beyond a point of land that juts off the ridge to the south of the lake. Some were lazily flapping from treetop to treetop among the aspen and black spruce. The whole

. . . .

The Snow Lotus

whirling and hopping flock was gradually progressing through the forest, approaching Secret Lake, and I should have realized what was happening. I suppose I was distracted by the seductive touch of that spring breeze.

As if to underscore my impression of winter's wake, a shaft of filtered sunlight pierced the overcast and painted a sheen of brightness on the wooded point. A few moments later I saw a German shepherd emerge from the trees, lightly stepping across the bog. My first reaction was irritation: whose damn dog was that wandering through the forest? Then three more "dogs"—in single file—abruptly appeared. Timberwolves! My heart skipped, and the frame of reference snapped from the mellow, soft-focus appreciation of warmth and butterflies to a keen-edged vigilance. I gaped. The ravens, as they often do, were shadowing a wolf pack.

The lead wolf—apparently an alpha male—was huge. Rev weighs about forty-five pounds, and this canine was at least twice his size. Its coat was a dappled gray, brown, and white that readily blended with the part snow/part bare ground of late winter, and if not for its silent motion it would've been difficult to spot against the backdrop of forest.

But then so was I: downwind and sitting low and still as a stump. The wolves were four hundred feet away and padding right for me; I was undetected. They were going to walk out onto the ice. How close would they get? I felt the Olympian joy of the invisible watcher.

Then I remembered The Reverend. He was a few yards behind me, sniffing around in the muskeg. When he got wind of the wolves—and he would—he was certain to charge. At the least he'd spook them, and the show would be over; at worst they'd trump his bluster and kill him. Damn! I didn't want to twitch a muscle, but I needed to collar The Rev.

I slowly rose to a crouch, hoping the wolves wouldn't notice, but realizing that was fantasy. My calculated stealth earned me about one full second of grace. The lead wolf froze, and for a moment we locked eyes. I'm sure the other three never saw me. The instant the alpha perked, they automatically veered away and literally turned tail, accelerating to a trot and vanishing into the woods.

The alpha started to follow them and I called Rev, but his nose was in the air. I hissed another sharp "Come!" that under normal circumstances would have immediately fetched him to my side. He ignored me. Tail high and hackles raised, he stormed after the wolves.

I began shouting and saw that the big alpha had merely scampered out of the open bog, then paused. It was standing on the rise of the point, at the edge of the trees but in full view, watching my bold and foolish dog. The wolf was now about five hundred feet away, the details of its face indiscernible, but its posture projecting an air of casual alertness. It was clearly *not* intimidated.

I was frantic. Each of my unheeded shouts to Rev grew louder and more strident, until the last was a near shriek. He'd closed about half the distance to the waiting alpha when my fear finally impressed him. He slowed, exuding reluctance, then came loping back to his own alpha.

As soon as The Reverend abandoned the challenge, the big wolf turned and ambled off. No hurry. I watched it weave through the trees for several seconds before it disappeared. The ravens, still squawking, followed, and their din gradually faded.

When Rev reached my side, I sank to one knee and hugged him. "Good dog! Good dog!" I intoned, lavishly rewarding the behavior (however grudging) that had possibly saved his life. As I playfully boxed his ears, I marveled that he and the big wolf were both *Canis lupus*, essentially the same species.

Nordic mythology features a monster-wolf, Fenris—son of Loki (another manifestation of Lucifer)—who could not be tethered with chains, and was eventually imprisoned deep in the earth. No dog that one. It was prophesied that at the end of the world—the Twilight of the Gods—the giant wolf will break from captivity and eat the sun.

.   .   .   .

The Snow Lotus

According to that article on solar evolution, the sun will expand dramatically before it finally collapses into a smoldering shadow of itself known as a white dwarf. About eight billion years from now it will be over 160 times its present size and, if conditions are right, may swell enough to consume the earth.

Thus, ancient mythology and modern astrophysics both speak of cosmic consumption, the destruction of heavenly bodies, which will include that of the beautiful Snow White, who will finally expire when all humans are extinct and there is no mind to imagine her. It's a pity she can't know that the climactic life stage of the sun is in the guise of a dwarf.

When I first studied astronomy some thirty years ago, and realized science believes that in one way or another the sun and the earth as we know them will eventually perish (how did the old Norse understand this? why create Fenris?), I was depressed. In the face of such potent cosmic fatalism, there was nothing I (we) could create as a human(s) that would not be destroyed—utterly, as if it (we) had never existed. So why bother to do anything? *All* our efforts, no matter how grand, are ultimately futile. Our species is doomed. The nature of our collective dark destiny makes the dinosaurs seem still vibrant; at least they left us fossilized bones.

To counter my depression I sought hope and consolation in religion, specifically the Roman Catholicism bequeathed to me at birth and mandated by early instruction. My *Baltimore Catechism* stated that people had immortal souls, and each soul was "a spiritual being, not dependent on matter, and hence not subject to decay or death." That was on page 131. On page 130 were listed the four sources of such truth: (1) God, (2) the Bible, (3) the Church, and (4) "We must use our own brain also." Presumably the first three must somehow be processed through the fourth, so over the years I used my brain a great deal—even earned a bachelor's degree in theology. And as warm and fuzzy as the notion of an immortal soul could be (unless, of course, you were condemned to be tortured by Satan in Hell for eternity), my brain could discern no evidence for it. I'm not categorically stating there is no immortal soul—it's pointless to debate a catechism. I've simply never been presented with proof. Given the nature of the question I'm fairly certain I never shall be. So trust in the soul if you desire, but after half a lifetime of questing I'm more inclined to believe in the death of the sun. I lay my money on Fenris.

But since I do not maintain a conviction of literal human immortality—no matter how sensuous the lips of the princess—I am still confronted with the question: Why bother to live this life? It is, after all, a lot of work. Believers in resurrection and survival beyond the grave are also so confronted; they merely delay the question until the "next" life.

The facile answer is that we just can't help it most of the time. The fundamental urge to breathe and feed is encoded in the fiber of our being. In the context of the work-a-day world my body is simply another biological system arching toward life as a plant reaches for the sun. The Reverend, I suspect, is happy with that, unquestioning of origins and ends, as content as a tree. He doesn't know any astrophysics. Spruce boughs do not whisper philosophy.

But humans cannot avoid it. We are enmeshed not only in the biosphere, but also in a complex ecology of ideas that support both joy and sorrow, euphoria and despair. We are bullied by acute self-awareness to negotiate a peace treaty with the cosmos—a peace of mind. The talks are often delicate, and we spend much time metaphorically arguing the shape of the conference table.

Nevertheless, we all hammer out a pact of some kind. My current philosophy is based on the apprehension that life is a poisoned apple and I am *not* Snow White. But I am often kissed—by perception and experience—and in those instants become aware of a brand of immortality. On April Fool's Day it was when I saw the first fluttering butterfly; it was when the alpha wolf and I locked eyes, implicitly acknowledging the mysterious gulf between species; it was when my beloved Reverend finally turned back to me. "It is eternity now," wrote Richard Jefferies. "I am in the midst of it. It is about me in the sunshine; I am in it as the butterfly in the light-laden air."

There is a Russian proverb that says, "Live with wolves, howl like a wolf." I'm convinced that if you focus on life, you will have more of it. Your intense awareness will cause time to expand—not in measurable duration, but in its capacity to carry joy.

It can't matter to an individual human that the sun and earth will die. My bright moments of life are, by their nature, timeless. They are braided into consciousness and memory for as long as my mind functions, and that will be for precisely as long as it is. What follows will be, by definition, completely irrelevant and inaccessible to the erstwhile perceiver called me. In that sense I am as eternal as a rock, as durable as the universe itself. That is immortal enough.

· · · · · · · · · · · · · · · · ·

Blue Velvet
Number Nine

I went to the woods because
I wished to live deliberately.
Thoreau

We understood that the black spruce planting site would punish us. The customary habitat of black spruce is wetland, and as Richard said when we first observed the site, "You know you're in trouble when you're planting trees next to marsh marigolds."

With intermittent help from Newman and couple of others, Richard and I had been "slamming in seedlings" at various locations for nine days. So far we'd been blessed. The weather was unseasonably cool, which held the mosquitoes and black flies at bay, and also conserved our sweat. While planting jack pine and white spruce up on the Dahlberg Road we had endured one eighty-five-degree afternoon that vividly reminded us what the seedling season could be like. Aggressive insects appeared as if spontaneously generated by solar radiation, and Newman was so badly sunburned that he almost puked. I had offered him some sunscreen in the morning, but he declined, so the next day we mercilessly mocked his suffering. Several days of tree planting can shine your mean streak.

We acknowledged, though, that it could be much worse. We weren't contract planters. As Minnesota Department of Natural Resources (DNR) "smokechasers"—seasonal wild-land firefighters—we were being paid an hourly wage, a relative luxury for woods work. In northern Minnesota the spring fire season and the tree planting season overlap, and May can be a hectic month. In their "spare" time, smoke-chasers often plant trees, or "future fuel" as we tend to think of it. However, most of the 120,000 seedlings in our DNR district were delegated to contractors who bid on the jobs and hired helpers. A typical bid is sixty to sixty-five dollars per thousand trees, so contract planters are acutely aware that each time a seedling is stuck in the ground, they gross about six cents. It's not that you can't earn a decent blue-collar wage while wielding a hoedad or a dibble bar, you just have to kill yourself to do it. As one might expect, it is not unusual to see Hispanic crews that have migrated to the northwoods for a few weeks—people accustomed to hard labor and dearly won dollars. They follow the tree-planting thermocline north from the Carolinas or Arkansas, and I do not envy their lifestyle.

We smokechasers are assigned the sites that contractors don't covet—small, scattered areas that would cramp their productivity. The black spruce site was one. It had been planted a few years before—unsuccessfully—and we had 1,500 seedlings to insert amid the few surviving trees. The DNR district forester speculated that it had been too dry the first time around, but it was clear that would not be a problem now. Standing water was visible in some spots, and I resigned myself to spongy socks.

And to the ticks. Just hiking the quarter mile into the site from the road had been sufficient to polka dot our pants with several ticks, any of which could be carrying Lyme disease. A couple days before we'd traded horror stories about the unfortunate folks we knew who had contracted the malady. A morbid discussion about arthritis, temporary paralysis, and massive drug therapies had served as a de facto ritual to ward off the evil from ourselves. I also tucked my pants into my boots, and sure enough, it kept the ticks off my legs. Instead, I was constantly plucking them from my neck. I suppose it was at least an inconvenience for the ticks to crawl that extra distance before striking exposed flesh.

The forecast was for sunshine and eighty degrees, so our strategy was to move fast/plant hard in the cool of the morning, and insert most of the black spruce by noon. We each filled a planting bag with prickly spruce seedlings, then stashed the two waxed cardboard tree boxes in the shade and under a reflective tarp. Printed on each box was "Handle With Care. Future Forest." and we took it to heart. Since we had our fire engine along in case of dispatch, we pulled out a pump can and sprayed the roots of the seedlings to help ensure their survival. Strapping the bags around our waists, we grabbed planting bars and marched into the swamp.

Richard was our grand old man when it came to planting—he'd performed contract work in his hungrier days—and he lined us out on the site, indicating how we'd traverse it, and acting as point man along the forest edge.

We were psyched up to be brisk, but the first time Richard thrust his bar into the ground we heard a dull "clunk," and he yelled, "Sex stone!" On our initial day of planting together I'd heard him shout "Sex stone!" a dozen times before I finally gave in.

"OK. What's the deal?"

He grinned. He'd been wondering how long it would take me to either figure it out or inquire.

. . . .

"A fucking rock!" he spat.

And so it was. Our black spruce ground consisted of three major components: thick moss, mounds of decaying logging slash, and sex stones. It really did help to yell or grunt each time you struck one; acknowledging the irritation and pain (it can be bone-jarring to hit a rock hard) kept it out in the open and partially defused the stress of a difficult site. It was vindictive terrain, highly resistant to planting bars. The moss was either dry and tough, or saturated mush; the slash was a tangled obstacle course. It seemed that for each seedling snugly planted, there were two or three abortive bar thrusts. Since the steel planting bar weighs about ten pounds, that extra energy drain sapped morale.

On a "clean" site one can easily develop an almost hypnotic rhythm: plunge the spade end of the bar into the soil, work it back and forth to create a slot, slip in a seedling (bending your knees instead of your back—if you're smart), jam the bar into the ground just behind the tree and push it forward to close the hole, then stomp the second hole with the heel of your boot to seal it and pack dirt around the tree. It's four basic steps to the seedling schottishe, and it looks easy and almost artistic when you're watching people perform it from a distance.

But complicating the choreography is the seedling itself. Long, stringy roots must end up straight in the ground. If you "J-plant" the tree, that is, if its roots curl up or are folded over in the hole, it'll probably expire. You pluck the tree out of the bag, note the length of the roots, and, if necessary, prune them with your fingers. If most of the seedlings in a given lot possess too much root mass for efficient planting, you can prune them in a bunch by laying them on the ground and chopping the ends with your bar. When you insert the tree into the hole, you push it all the way to the bottom then pull it back up to straighten the roots, making sure not to plant it too deep or too shallow. The foresters will check every site, and a sloppy performance stands out.

.   .   .   .

Thus, it's not a completely mindless task, though an inspection of our hands would have revealed the essence of the job. After several days exposed to the constant friction of conifer needles, dirt, and cold steel, my palms were calloused, my knuckles cracked and bleeding, my pores packed with soil. Each night's vigorous handwashing had little effect, and Richard suggested I wait until the planting was done before I wasted a lot of time trying to make my skin look and feel normal. He mentioned that at the end of other seasons he had used sandpaper to dress up his hands. For a few minutes that morning we actually discussed the merits of various brands of lotion—like TV housewives in a detergent commercial.

By 10:00 A.M. the sun was hot and the black flies were biting. Despite our intentions, and nine days of seasoning, our progress was phlegmatic, and it was evident that this measly batch of 1,500 trees was going to require five or six hours of toil. We chattered incessantly to pass the time, our talk running the gamut from clucking over the Branch Davidian affair unfolding in Waco, Texas, to local firefighters' gossip; from hand cream and woodticks to Bill Clinton's BTU tax. We told jokes, indulged in a lot of recreational bitching, and occasionally sang to ourselves when the conversation lapsed. We tended to quiet down and draw inward as the heat rose and fatigue began to stalk us, our weariness steadily evolving across the hours until I realized we were all a little testy, and what banter remained had an edge to it.

We hiked back out to the truck for lunch, dividing the break between sandwiches and tick plucking. Food provided a lift, and we turned on the radio to catch some news and music. We tuned in to an "all-request oldies show," and at one point a female caller asked the DJ to "please play 'Blue Velvet Number Nine.'" The jockey laughed. "Well," he said, "which is it?" There was embarrassed giggling on the line, and the woman replied, "Oh! I always get those two mixed up; I guess I want to hear 'Love Potion Number Nine,' and please dedicate that to . . ." But we were already hearing, "I

· · · · · · · · · · · · · · · ·

took my troubles down to Madam Ruth / You know that gypsy with the gold-capped tooth. . . ."

I chuckled. "Blue Velvet Number Nine" had poetic resonance to it—wasn't a real title, but should be. Back out on the site an hour later it came to mind again, and I decided that the confused, out-of-sync title the caller had inadvertently created evoked the nature of our work. First, we were firefighters planting trees, attired in our green Nomex pants and yellow Nomex shirts, with me packing a portable two-way radio. We didn't look like migrant laborers. But second, and more important, was the recollection of a passage from Thoreau that I had just read the day before. A Minneapolis weekly newspaper had assigned me to review *Faith in a Seed: The First Publication of Thoreau's Last Manuscript,* and on the first page of a section entitled "The Dispersion of Seeds," I read:

> We are so accustomed to see another forest spring up immediately, as a matter of course, when one is cut down (whether from stump or from seed), never troubling ourselves about the succession, that we hardly associate seeds with trees, and do not anticipate the time when this regular succession will cease and we shall be obliged to plant, as they do in all old countries.

I smiled and immediately read the passage to Pam. I brandished my tortured hands and said, "I guess we live in an old country."

That hot afternoon, as Richard, Newman, and I struggled around slash piles to set our trees in gardenlike rows, I mused on the artificial tone of our project. There are forests and there are tree plantations; they are both groups of trees, but they aren't the same thing—not by a long shot.

We had talked about it on our first day of planting, how a large pine plantation—say, over forty acres—is a biological desert compared to natural woods, and how we were glad to be working the small sites hemmed in by real forest, and could thus feel less guilty about purposely introducing a

.   .   .   .

The Snow Lotus

monoculture into an ecosystem that thrives on diversity. (One bright fact for the seasonal firefighter is that plantations often burn quite furiously, providing us both stimulation and income.) In the course of that discussion I had picked up another rueful bit of planters' jargon. Some foresters and loggers refer to the cutting of timber as "greasing"—as in "we greased that stand of aspen." The roots of the term pertain, of course, to killing, and I thought of the "grease gun," an American-made submachine gun of the World War II era. "Greasing" connotes violent death, and is perhaps apt for a logging operation.

But, Richard observed, if the timber harvest is "greasing," then our planting was *"de-*greasing," and he fondly used the word every day. For me it instantly conjured up a ludicrous image of the three of us bent over freshly cut pine stumps, grasping stiff-bristled brushes. We dip them into bubbly pails of surfactants, and vigorously scrub the stumps, obliterating any trace of chain-saw bar oil or roller-nose lubricant.

Degreasing. I wasn't as enamored of the term as Richard obviously was, but I could see the intent. It was a direct confrontation of the crude "greasing"—birth versus death, green versus brown—and if you considered a particular logging operation to be offensive (many are, many are not), then "degreasing" was a double negative that equaled a positive, a pleasing incongruity—like "Blue Velvet Number Nine."

We finished the black spruce site around 2:00 P.M., and trudged out of the woods with gloriously empty tree bags. We drove to Riverside Inn for some malts, and were just priming the straws when the dispatcher hailed us on the radio. There was a snappy forest fire near Mountain Iron, and we should proceed there immediately. With our engine's light bar flashing overhead, we sped down Highway 5, sucking on malts, joyful to have a fire and grateful to be rid of spruce seedlings. I felt more vibrant as a firefighter than as a tree planter, and certainly more excited. But in the midst of our planting I had seen a wonderful thing.

.   .   .   .

At one point I had jammed my bar into the soil, and there was an explosion of wings. I reared back like a startled horse, then froze. It was a woodcock, and several days earlier we had seen a clutch of eggs on the ground at another site. I didn't want to step on any. The woodcock flew only a few yards and fell into a broken wing routine, attempting to draw me away from the nest. I surveyed the earth at my feet, but saw no eggs. A subtle movement caught my eye, and I abruptly focused on two tiny chicks — a pair of delicate feather balls with long beaks, so effectively camouflaged that when I briefly glanced away at their mother I had a difficult time spotting them again, even though neither they nor I had budged. I pointed them out to Richard, and he stared for several seconds to make them out. We quickly moved on, noting the location so we could allow it a wide berth for the rest of the day.

During decades of living in the woods I had never seen woodcock chicks, and it was an unexpected gift, a moment of revelation. If I hadn't nearly hit the birds with my planting bar, they would have remained undiscovered — their aim, of course, but I was satisfied no harm was done.

I just hoped they — and we — can thrive in an old country.

The Cosmos
and Lysistrata

The words of my book nothing, the drift of it everything.
WALT WHITMAN

I blinked at a universe down in the bog. It was an early
morning in late May, and the temperature had been near
frost at dawn, about thirty-four degrees. A pregnant dew collapsed out of the ether, heavy as rainfall, and the labrador
tea and leatherleaf were beaded and brilliant.

Streaming from just over the spruce tops, sunlight glutted
the bog, and I was dazzled by thousands of spiderwebs. They
were mostly small, two to three inches in diameter, and
seemed to occupy every available notch and twig. The dwarf
birch, the tea, the leatherleaf, even higher clumps of sphagnum moss, were thickly clad with dew-spangled webs. They

were concentrated knots of intersecting threads, globular tangles of glistening silk.

I was reminded of a June profusion of cotton flowers, like tiny clots of cloud in a microcosm of the summer sky. But the sparkling lenses of dew, like tens of thousands of tiny glass chips, were suddenly resolved as stars. From this god-like perspective I could see the webs as galaxies, tight clusters of suns spread out before me in a vast volume of outer space. I imagined myself as an intergalactic navigator approaching the rim of the Virgo Supercluster, an aggregation of galaxies—or "island universes," as they were once called—so stupendous that the mind falters to contemplate it.

This three-acre expanse of spiderwebs was startling, marvelous, and I was compelled to elevate it to the heavens. I made a representative count and estimated I could see about four thousand "galaxies." I sipped my coffee, then raised the mug and whispered, "Good morning, Cosmos."

It was amazing enough to realize that small arthropods had deliberately engineered these webs to capture other creatures, but one of the joys of intelligence is to consider every phenomenon as more than one thing. Metaphor and simile are the lifeblood of mind, and I honored the spiders by imagining them as crafters of island universes. (And perhaps to spiders, that's precisely what webs are.)

A couple of weeks later, in mid-June, Pam and I hauled our canoe to a small, clear lake known for its teeming population of largemouth bass. I portaged the canoe down a path between birch and red pine, and we gently pushed off through a bouquet of purple irises that grew in the shallows. As I eased along, barely paddling, Pam dispatched the first elegant cast with her handmade fly rod. A green popper plunked amid some reeds next to a half-sunken deadfall.

"Why don't you keep track," she said.

The action in that lake is usually so frenetic that it amuses us to tally her casts and the number of fish caught (and released) per minute spent on the water.

. . . .

The Snow Lotus

I noted the start time, and on her second cast Pam hooked the first bass. Though only eight inches long, it fought like a lunker, bending the rod and leaping clear of the surface before tiring next to the canoe. Pam usually directs the fish toward the stern where I can grasp the line, pull it in, quickly grab the catch, remove the hook, and release the fish. They almost always dive straight for the bottom. Pam doesn't mind handling the fish herself, but this method is faster, and thus better for the fish, plus I have the opportunity to be intimately involved. We both admire the iridescent sheen of bass scales during their brief exposure to the sky.

The water is so transparent that every submarine feature down to a dozen feet is clearly visible. Even from thirty feet away and five feet above, we could see the beds where the bass eggs had been laid—bare patches of gravel on the bottom that they'd swept clear of vegetation and debris. These beds are jealously guarded, and nearly every time Pam drew the popper over a bed—ostentatiously jerking it along—a bass would rise to strike. We spied them stalking the lure before their final lunge, and it was like floating on the surface of a giant aquarium.

One cast startled a painted turtle that was sunning itself on a rock, and it plopped into the water and swam for the bottom. I watched its every stroke—stubby legs shoving like misshapen oars—until it settled beneath a log.

We glided past four beaver lodges, and actually heard a loud munching noise before we spotted a beaver straddling a partially submerged aspen trunk. It had been recently felled, and the beaver was vigorously limbing and debarking. As we drew near it seemed reluctant to leave the tree that doubled as buffet and lumber yard. It stiffened and eyed us, but resumed chewing. We crept within ten yards before the beaver slid off and swam across our bow. It was big, possibly thirty pounds or more, and when it slapped its tail and dove, a plume of water shot up six or seven feet.

A storm front had been slowly rolling in from the west, and when the sun was finally masked by dark clouds, we

. . . .

had circumnavigated the lake. We flushed a pair of mergansers out of the irises as we put into shore, and in a flurry of splashing they pounded the water with their wings, lifted into the air, and banked out of sight around a point. It didn't seem they intended to fly far; rough weather was signaled by the cool breeze now ruffling the surface.

Before I hoisted the canoe to my shoulders I announced the final tally. In ninety-three minutes Pam had made 202 casts and caught fifty-one bass; a fish every four minutes, and she'd hooked several more that managed to spit the hook. An hour and a half of fishing seems a small matter, and utterly routine in this part of the world, but we left the lake in a state of mind at once energized and composed, like ardent believers after a particularly moving church service. I won't delve into the cliché of fishing as ritual (especially fly fishing), but we felt that no matter what transpired for the balance of the day, we had experienced ninety-three full and precious minutes, and a nexus with the natural world. Like the "cosmos" of spiderwebs, our fishing excursion was more than one thing, and an easy paddle around a small lake can be a long journey.

About a month later I was staying in a small rural community in Idaho when a theater troupe arrived. An outdoor performance was planned, but rain forced a last minute move into an empty commercial building, where about seventy-five of us sat in a rough semicircle of folding chairs. With no stage, the actors and their props shared our floor, our level, and it was surprisingly intimate—as if we'd gathered in a large family room.

The play was *Lysistrata* by K. Michael Levine, and the cast was magnificent—their obvious talent amplified by our hunger for something different. Live drama in backwoods Idaho is about as rare as a noncontroversial timber sale.

I noticed several small children in the audience, and I supposed their parents intended to expose them to "culture" whether they fully appreciated it or not. I wondered about that; I assumed the kids would be bored. *Lysistrata* is adult fare, an intense tragedy. The title character is a woman drawn into a fervent antiwar movement. She proposes that the women of Athens deny sex to their partners until the grievous combat with Sparta is ended. The idea gains momentum, and the military fights the organized outrage of the women. The play unflinchingly explores the nature of state authority, gender politics, and personal morality. At one point, Lysistrata is brutally interrogated and tortured, and within the close atmosphere of our "family room," it was painful to watch.

In the loud and feverish final scene, with the actors projecting at full power, Lysistrata suffered her anguished, tragic death, and the play was over. As we all rose to applaud, a young girl—perhaps four or five years old—burst into pathetic sobs. She had not been bored, but transfixed; she apparently believed that Lysistrata, played by a warm and pretty actress, truly had died before her eyes.

Lysistrata leaped up from the floor and strode among the chairs. Smiling and cooing, she picked up the little girl and assured her that all was well. She hugged and rocked her, and the rest of the cast gathered to contribute their solace. In a few moments the youngster was beaming through her tears.

By then I was blinking back my own. Watching the girl's sobbing transformed into swift, building joy, awakened in me explicit recollections of overwhelming childhood terrors—surgery at an early age; the commonplace anxiety that Mom, out for the evening, would be killed in a car accident; the regular searing nightmares featuring goblins and sea monsters. And for a fleeting moment I shared in the girl's immense relief and soaring happiness. I remembered how that felt: my hospital ordeal had ended; Mom returned home; and there was the genuine, vivifying rapture of waking up and realizing that the giant, coiling python was merely a bad dream.

In the program there was an author's note from Mr. Levine: "*Lysistrata* is no more about war, sex, and gender than chocolate cake is about eggs, yeast, and flour." And in the mirror of a little girl's tears—backlit with a smile—I glimpsed my own childhood heartaches and joys. And tears, of course, are like dewdrops on spiderwebs, and they all percolate down to a lake full of largemouth bass and painted turtles.

· · · · · · · · · · · · · · · · ·

ᔕ A Damn Idiot

.
.
.
.
.
.
.
.
.
.
.

Heartleaf arnica spreads from extensive underground roots, does not crowd itself. . . .
LEE STRICKLER

It was a wet summer in Idaho's Nez Perce National Forest, and the mountains were ripe with wildflowers. In a meadow above Fish Creek I was cheered by flecks and clusters of color—red, yellow, blue, violet, orange—against a lush backdrop of multiple shades of green encompassed by a cloud-speckled sky. There was a bee hovering on nearly every blossom, and they generated a pervasive hum that seemed a vibration of the air itself.

Though I had recently cataloged fifty-three species of wildflowers on our forty acres of woods back in Minnesota (and expected to find many more), the Nez was virgin territory, and I eagerly thumbed through my newly purchased field guide to the northern Rocky Mountain states. In a few minutes I could identify golden pea, rose pussytoes, queen's cup, small-flowered penstemon, black-headed coneflowers, and a half-dozen others. I was delighted, thoroughly engaged by these fresh wonders, and also glad to find some of the same flowers that lived in the forests of home—yarrow, wild rose, dandelion, strawberry, cinquefoil.

I was clambering upslope toward yet another clump of enticing strangers when I found half the jaw of a long-dead elk. I automatically picked it up, as surely as I would have at age seven; I've always been fascinated by bones and skeletons discovered in the woods. Most of the teeth were gone, and I hastily replaced the jaw when I realized it was sheltering a colony of red ants. Twenty feet farther on I spotted the opposite half of the jaw, and another time I might have joined the two and studied them against the sky.

But these decaying bones shattered my mood. The image of death, however natural and appropriate in that sylvan meadow, forcefully reminded me of the day's events. Why was I hunting wildflowers, rambling that ridgeline like a carefree child? Why hadn't I just retreated to my rented trailer and slunk into bed? Only a short time earlier my impulse had been to hurry there and draw the covers over my face.

My first day off since arriving in Grangeville, Idaho, for a seasonal Forest Service firefighting job had begun well. I enjoyed a brisk workout at the base; the weather was gorgeous, and on the spur of the moment over morning coffee I decided to transfer my wildflower hobby to the Nez Perce forest. I needed a field guide, and I figured the quaint little bookstore downtown was bound to stock one. But as I walked the mile or so through town, I encountered three disturbing scenes in a matter of minutes.

First was the nursing home yard. An old man was sunk in a lawn chair, his spine crooked with age. He was bent over nearly double, and the only thing he could see was his lap. His face was pinched and sallow, pale as a cadaver, and I easily imagined him in a casket. He had a pair of visitors—I guessed an adult daughter and a grandson—and I heard him mumbling, speaking at his thighs. I had no proof this man was miserable, but the obvious ravages of life and time suddenly struck me as an immutable vision of the future. It was possible, perhaps probable, that his decrepitude would be mine. At age forty-two I was already feeling stabs of arthritis, deteriorating discs, a damaged knee. I looked away.

Three blocks farther on I saw a middle-aged woman leaning on a planter at a street corner. There was a worn knapsack slouched at her feet, and she clutched a sign made of dirty cardboard. She held it up for passersby to read: "Hungry. Out of money, out of gas. Please help."

I debated as I approached. I wasn't exactly flush with cash myself. Why else would I be working for $8.79 per hour 1,400 miles from home? And maybe this woman was just a panhandler and not truly gripped by emergency. But she appeared genuine, and I was on an errand to spend several dollars on a wildflower field guide—a frivolous purchase in light of her apparent need. I quickly rifled through the bills in my wallet as I walked, judged the distance to my first payday, and pulled out a fiver. I passed it to her without a word as I strode by, and she whispered, "God bless you!" There was pathos in it, and I didn't look back. I felt guilty for debating, then guilty for feeling guilty, then simply embarrassed by it all.

The familiar smell of the bookstore—of unthumbed pages and fresh bindings—was a tonic, and yes, there was a good field guide and I bought it immediately. I would hurry up to the crisp mountain air.

But on the way back to my trailer, just past the nursing home (the old man was gone), I saw a retarded adult walk into the middle of the street. Though tall and husky with an ample potbelly, he was dressed as a tyke—T-shirt, shorts, tenners, and knee socks. He walked with exaggerated precision, like a cadet on parade, back plumb, each movement executed as if consciously planned. There were three dead tree limbs in the street, and he halted by one, slowly bent his knees, and picked it up. He straightened, stepped to the next, bent his knees, picked it up. And so with the third. The sequence was robotic and solemn, almost liturgical. This big boy with Down's syndrome had lent such gravity to the simple, menial task that I was abruptly awash in sadness to see it. How many times had he been ridiculed or shunned as he was growing up, been taunted with "sissy" or "waterhead"? Maybe, of course, never; I didn't know him, nor any details of his life. But he thrust the branches straight out in front of him, like a priest with a censer, and marched toward a garbage can in the alley behind his house. Did he consider that job as important as he made it appear? If so, was that good or bad? Was his life incredibly narrow, circumscribed by simple chores writ large, or incredibly rich, with profound meaning suffusing dead branches in the street? I could not tell in walking by. I hoped for the latter, but doubted it; then chided myself for being pessimistic, and innately smug over my own good fortune. I had not been born with burdens that other humans would ensure that I carried.

In a few minutes I was in my pickup, heading out of town on the Mount Idaho Road. I spotted a hitchhiker with a huge backpack. It was a narrow highway with minimal shoulders, so I pulled over in a private driveway near the base of a hill. The hiker trotted up, but we soon discovered we were bound for separate ways at the next junction, which was only a quarter mile ahead. "Thanks anyway," he said.

I glanced in my rearview mirror at the crest of the hill behind and saw nothing. I turned out into the road. Just as I drove off, an elderly man on a motorcycle shot over the top of the hill and saw me enter the lane in front of him. We were only several yards apart and he was doing about thirty-five miles per hour. At that point I checked my mirror again and saw the cycle. Its front wheel was jerking violently from side to side as the man frantically braked, swerved, and lost control. My guts surged: this guy was going to be hurt. I spun to the right to clear the way, but the bike toppled over into the left lane and skidded into the weeds. The rider pitched off the seat and rolled on the asphalt.

I lurched to a stop and flung open the door, but the man was already on his feet. He tore off his helmet and bellowed at me, "You goddamn idiot!"

His shirt and jeans were ripped, and I saw blood on both his arms. He looked to be about sixty years old and I was surprised by his energy. His face was contorted with rage and the residue of terror. He was big, and I thought he might punch me, but I hurried over to face him, speaking before he could shout again, "Oh man! I'm sorry!"

The hitchhiker had also run over, and the biker calmed as quickly as he'd cursed. I half pleaded for his pardon. "I just didn't *see* you," I said. He shook his head in disgust and I sprinted to a nearby house and asked a teenager to phone 911.

While waiting for the police, the hitchhiker and I helped the man—we introduced ourselves, his name was Joe—pick up his motorcycle and push it across the road into a driveway. Some of Joe's blood was smeared on my right hand, and I belatedly remembered the latex gloves I kept in my glove compartment for just such an emergency. By the time an ambulance and squad car arrived about five minutes later, Joe was in good spirits—considering—and we chatted about how it could have been much worse.

"Thank god you were wearing a helmet," I said.
"Yeah!"

But I was devastated. What I had done wasn't idiotic, but I shouldn't have been parked below the crest of hill, nor relied solely on my mirror to check the rear. The mishap was part bad luck—we'd both been in the wrong place at the wrong time—but it certainly wasn't Joe's fault, and his initial anger was justified. If he had smacked into my truck he could easily have been killed. As the deputy filled out his

.   .   .   .

accident report, I was queasy with shame. I worked on a
helicopter crew during the Idaho fire season, and prided
myself on being alert and safety conscious—that is, professional—not only for my sake, but also for all the firefighters who followed my direction at helispots and on the
fireground. But my carelessness had caused this accident,
and I suddenly doubted my worth. I knew that was an over-
reaction to the stress at hand, but the realization failed to
make me (or Joe) feel any better.

Joe refused an ambulance ride, and the deputy gave him a
lift home. Before they left, Joe said he was going to have his
son come by with a truck to retrieve the motorcycle. I offered to stick around and help load—it was a big bike—but
he said that wouldn't be necessary. So partial expiation was
denied me.

When they were gone the hitchhiker stated for the third
time that he felt responsible also (he'd even said so to the
police), and for the third time I absolved him of the guilt I
had fully laid on myself—except for the little I assigned to
fate. The hiker was bound for Elk City and Montana beyond,
and I wished him a good journey.

I sat in my truck for several minutes, wondering what to
do. The new field guide mocked me from the dashboard.
The wildflower mission that was so fresh and seductive only
a half hour before seemed misbegotten and trivial. A man
was injured, and he could have died because I had neglected
to exercise care. I felt like going home to weep—not only
"home" to the trailer, but all the way to Minnesota. The
image of Joe yanking off his helmet was still vivid. "You
goddamn idiot!"

Then I thought of the old man talking into his lap, the
beggar with the cardboard sign, the retarded man/boy grasping his precious branches. So much in the world I couldn't
control—even this damn remorse that made wildflowers
seem like shit! And one thing I did control—making ab-

.   .   .   .

solutely sure no one was behind me when I turned my vehicle into a roadway—I had fumbled. "You goddamn idiot!"

Nevertheless, I understood that the best thing to do was drive on.

With extra caution, and even trembling a bit, I pulled onto the highway and headed for the mountains. I would use my new field guide. I had to face the rest of the day, and self-pity in bed was a luxury I could not afford. I hadn't counted enough cash in my wallet to go home, and, after all, I was better off than most folks I'd seen that day—at least for now.

I drove to a favorite meadow and rinsed Joe's blood in a puddle, wiping my hand on moist clover. Several minutes later, when I found the elk jaw, I was paralyzed for only a moment. I forced myself to keep hunting, and was rewarded with my first glimpse of a heartleaf arnica, a yellow burst of life on the forest floor that I only detected by hunkering low and paying attention. Soon I was immersed in the delicate grace of blossoms, leaves, and stems all around, and a couple of hours later I realized the worth of field guides: they bend your focus to something besides yourself.

Wildflowers bloom everywhere—mountain glades and bogs, roadside ditches and deep woods, stream banks and ledge-rock crevices. They are as important as shame; and a great deal more potent than pity.

·   ·   ·   ·   ·   ·   ·   ·   ·   ·   ·   ·   ·   ·   ·

⑨ Washing the Sky
to Amber

But these are just golden dreams.
DOSTOYEVSKY, Notes from Underground

One sizzling afternoon, as we hunkered down in "the black"
next to a charred deadfall, The G-Man said, "Every day out
here has at least one *moment.*"

I nodded, reckoning the slow hours of monotony and
drudgery that are often the most formidable challenge of a
wildfire crew. Contrary to vivid impressions offered by the
media, boredom is more customary than terror, yawns as potent as adrenaline. "It all pays the same" is a proverb of the
fire grunt, but it's easier to dig line, drenched in sweat, than
to stand by—waiting, waiting—for transportation, for deci-

sions, for the fire to lie down. It often seems that most of our time is consumed bumping along in buses or trucks, fidgeting in line for meals or an empty privy, patrolling for unlikely hot spots on cold mountainsides.

But yes, there's usually *the moment*. On that fire in central Washington, a 125,000-acre monster called Tyee Creek, my moment for Day 8 arrived late in the shift. Earlier—around noon—in soul-sapping ninety-five-degree heat, we had hiked up a long 75 percent slope, gagging on kicked-up clouds of ankle-deep dust. At the summit we endured several hours of cutting line around spot fires, with torching firs intensifying the heat of our localized purgatory. It hurt—deep in the chest, and on every square inch of the face. Nevertheless, there was genuine purpose, and it was almost *the moment*—probably would have been if not upstaged by that brief, downslope passage into the sunset.

At this point it helps to know Y. T. He's a combat veteran of Vietnam, and a while back we shared a fire detail in Idaho. One afternoon our conversation ranged into the topic of war movies, and Y. T. expressed scorn—not only the usual indictments of unreality and glorification, but also because of his particular experience. He was a member of a Long Range Reconnaissance Patrol (LRRP), a unit that was usually delivered via helicopter deep into hostile territory, and left there for days at a time. Their chief mission was silence. They might lay in one spot for an entire day—not moving, not speaking, not eating or smoking—shunning any activity that could arouse the senses of the enemy. Infrequent communication was accomplished with discreet hand signals. Y. T. told me that his memories of the war are dominated not by the staple cinematic racket of explosions and gunfire (though he's missing a kneecap to prove that he experienced his share of dramatic noise), but by the profound quiet of the recon patrol. Even when traveling, it was in a forcefield of silence, each step measured against the potential of ambush, booby traps, snakebite. It might require hours to cover distance that could be conveniently tallied in meters. Despite the deadly ordeal of killing and almost being killed, Y. T. lucidly recalls and emphasizes the protracted stretches of nonheroic silence.

And so too, as I remember the great Tyee Creek fire, the image that surfaces most prominently is the Day 8 sundown. Maybe the priority of memories is established by surprise, by the unexpected moments that cut against the grain of personal and popular preconception. To be sure, Y. T. will not forget the firefights, but he speaks more wonderingly of the quiet that will never form the nucleus of a movie.

The G-Man was right behind me on Day 8 as we angled off the crest of Slide Ridge and headed down the line that cut for the road almost a mile below. Despite physical weariness I felt buoyant. Our crew had held a section of line considered untenable the day before, and that was almost sacrificed to the fire. My brain was enriched with the righteous biochemicals exuded in the wake of strenuous exertion overlaid by awareness of danger. Just three or four steps from the crest I knew I had encountered *the moment*. In a surge of elation, my vitality was wed to that niche of the world.

I was struck first by the panorama of light and the exalted sweep of landscape. The sun, westering and tarnished by smoke, had washed the sky to amber. In a wide-angle span from northeast to south to northwest, the tawny range of forested peaks and saddles—some burned off and still puffing—seemed to swell up just across the drainage, then gradually roll away to the horizon like waves on a fantastical sea. Silhouetted against a column of brindled smoke, a helicopter hovered above a hot spot about a mile away, hanging there briefly like a raptor riding the thermals. On the opposite slope of the valley I saw a sinuous string of firefighters, a band of our brothers and sisters—their yellow shirts bright specks of flux amid the hecatomb of snags.

I had a chain saw riding on my left shoulder, a Pro Mac 700, with a set of chaps wrapped around the bar to shield me from the cutters. It was almost perfectly balanced, and only the lightest grip of my fingertips on the roller nose kept it snugly against my neck, even on the steep descent. It was twenty extra pounds, but I was devoted to that weight, a burden of pride, but also of bemusement. Twenty-one years before, in the summer of 1973, I had slaved on a logging crew in the Oregon Cascades. It was dry in July and August, and an outbreak of wildfires had raised the possibility that we'd be forced to cease our timber operations and join the fire suppression effort. I knew nothing of firefighting then, except what I had seen in newspapers and on television, but the prospect engendered daydreams out on the landing. Battling forest fires seemed far more glamorous than logging, and in my youthful craving for adventure and attention, I imagined myself on the cover of *Time* magazine, picturing the details to help pass the long hours in the woods: my face blackened by soot, but bravely grinning into the camera with a big chain saw slung over my shoulder; I was slogging up a mountainside at the head of a column of firefighters against a backdrop of burned forest.

By the end of that summer the vainglorious image was forgotten, until fourteen years later in 1987 when, with a startled sensation of déjà vu, I found myself in precisely that situation — in Oregon no less! The reality fit the old daydream to a literally hair-raising degree, except there were no photographers from the national media to record the grin that lit my face when I realized I was actually living a fantasy. I wondered — had that conjured image of August 1973 directed my life choices in some subconscious way to ensure its fulfillment? It could have been coincidence, but felt grander. To end up on a fire crew in Oregon at age thirty-six was an unlikely prospect, and certainly not consciously planned nor anticipated. A sharp awareness of fate and destiny yoked the chain saw to my shoulder, and likewise on the trail off Slide Ridge. The images of '73 and '87 reemerged full force, and I smiled — still crazy after all these years, still walking the realm of wishes.

.   .   .   .

The Snow Lotus

The heels of my lug-soled boots gouged into the loose sand and gravel of the trail, and despite laborious line cutting and the load of chain saw and fire pack, there was no pain in my arthritic ankle—the one that was crushed and nearly destroyed in an industrial accident in 1972. It always aches on a downslope hike, but not that day. There are few delights so lusty as the absence of expected pain. It's a void of substance; the closet where there is no bogeyman, the X ray showing no fracture. Without the pain, I grasped a second wind, and a conviction that I controlled boundless energy, that assumptions of prowess were not ridiculous. I recalled the altered states of mind my collegiate distance running partners and I had often attained out on the fifteen-mile course so many years ago. "I can fly!" we'd yell, and "No pain! No pain!" Yes! My mind was charged and every impression was acute.

The air was perfumed by the rough-edged fragrance of labor, a blend of woodsmoke, bar oil, and sooty sweat. It might have been too pungent in, say, a restaurant or an airport terminal, but on the flank of Slide Ridge, occasionally mixed with a draught of fresh alpine atmosphere, it was a galvanic aroma that seemed entwined with the ambient melodies. These notes were the cadences of toil, the rasp of my breath embellished by the squeak and rustle of web gear—mine and that of the nineteen firefighters following—all reconciled with the soft background of an upslope breeze in the fir boughs, and the sporadic coughing that is our trademark.

I tasted the dust and smoke—earthy, acrid, and nearly as tangy as the dip of Copenhagen snuff bulging in my lip. My right eye was stinging with sweat, but I was happy, as glad and jubilant as I've ever been. I started to sing a poignant Iris Dement tune that I learned only a few months before (the G-Man was used to spontaneous outbursts by now): "Sweet is the melody, so hard to come by . . ." And yet, so easy. To attain this abruptly blissful moment I had done nothing but earnestly live and move in the place where

.   .   .   .

I was. On the other hand, the trail to Slide Ridge had been rugged and harrowing. Paradoxically, I had earned this free gift.

I was reminded of this about halfway down to the road, when we passed The Stump. Two days earlier, before the fire had reached Slide Ridge, our crew was assigned to "improve the line" just punched in by a bulldozer. With hand tools and my chain saw, we waded into thick woods on the fire side of the line, lopping limbs and felling trees to reduce the fuel load. We were at it for twenty or thirty minutes when the crew boss hailed me and pointed to a majestic Douglas fir on the opposite side of the line. "That'll have to come down," he said. Its expansive crown of highly flammable needles could easily compromise our position if it was ignited by airborne embers.

My swamper, Mark, and I trudged up to the old giant and craned our necks to study the top. Clearly, it was leaning in exactly the wrong direction, and would demand some fancy cutting and wedging to topple it on the proper side of the line. Mark is a professional logger in the real world, and I deferred to his judgment. He described a procedure I had never attempted. The G-Man, who had joined our discussion at the base of the tree, was skeptical, but it sounded worth trying to me. I filed a fresh edge onto the cutters of the Pro Mac, topped off the fuel tank, and fired it up. Under Mark's watchful eye I notched the side of the tree facing our proposed direction of fall, cutting about a third of the way through the trunk. That was the easy part.

Supporting the heavy saw at chest level and hoping that my footing held in the loose soil, I eased the nose of the bar straight into the bark, about two inches above and behind the back of the notch, burrowing in until the saw was buried to the "hilt." The twenty-four-inch bar wasn't long enough to push out the opposite side of the trunk, so I repeated the operation from that side to match up with the first plunge cut. Following Mark's gestured instructions, I then fanned out the pair of plunge cuts to the back of the trunk—until

. . . .

The Snow Lotus

they almost met—but left a small spine of "holding wood" to prevent the tree from dropping before we could wedge it toward the notch.

Mark quickly jammed a ten-inch plastic wedge on either side of the spine, and hammered them in as far as possible with the flat head of his ax. I shut down the Mac and took a breather, my arms rubbery after clutching the saw for several minutes of tense, above-the-waist cutting. I was keenly aware that we had an audience (the rest of the crew), and also that such a massive tree was extremely hazardous if it twisted off the stump the wrong way. As I took a long swig from my canteen, Mark explained our final move. I would carefully undercut that spine, and he would pound the wedges. Theoretically, the huge fir would slowly lean over, closing the notch, then tip past the point of no return. Meanwhile, we'd scamper away at a forty-five-degree angle to the direction of the drop.

I restarted the saw, undercut the holding wood, and ducked to the side as Mark deftly and vigorously struck the wedges—first one, then the other. Unfortunately, I had inadvertently undercut one of the wedges as well, effectively creating a larger kerf for Mark to expand. If not for that, I believe the fir would have tipped over after three or four blows. As it was, Mark quickly delivered over a dozen, and both wedges were fully embedded, flush with the bark. I backed off to watch the top of the tree, and it did budge, canting from a lean to a plumb position, but not yet tipping. Stalemate.

It was then that G-Man shouted, "Listen!"

Mark stopped swinging and we heard it instantly—the terrible roar of a fire making a serious run. It sounded like a storm wind, or an approaching jet aircraft, and it was directly downslope.

"Let's go!" yelled G-Man. As a hotshot crew veteran, his opinion was golden. It was apparent that Slide Ridge would be burned over in a few minutes—or less, who could tell for sure? Here was one of G-Man's *moments*.

.   .   .   .

Mark and I locked eyes, realizing we both knew that we could *not* leave the huge fir hanging like a booby trap. A stampeding fire rolling upslope is a merciless killer, but falling trees maim and slay a surprising number of firefighters, and we have all been endlessly drilled in the hazards of snags. Though it happens occasionally, I've never personally met anyone who was seriously burned in a wildfire, but I know two people who were crippled by falling snags. To leave that tree standing flew in the face of all my experience and sensibilities. And yet, we were about to be overrun by fire—big fire—the howl was rising like a nightmare wail and smoke was cresting the treetops just below the ridgeline. Without a word Mark launched into a frenzy of blows, chips of bark flying like shrapnel as he hammered the wedges further into the trunk. I was painfully aware that my careless undercut had forged our predicament, but it suddenly occurred to me that it no longer mattered which way the tree fell since the line was obviously doomed. If I cut the initial notch deeper, the fir might fall immediately in the direction we'd been trying to avoid. So what? At least it would be down.

"Let's go!" the G-Man insisted again. I was about to yank on the starter rope of the Mac when I saw the top of the fir begin to lean. "It's going!" I shouted. Mark's pounding had become savage as the fire filled our ears, and he swung twice more and stepped back. The fir was tilting. We ran out to the middle of the dozer line and paused for a few seconds to watch the tree plummet. There was a crack like a gunshot when it tore away from the stump, and it crashed to the ground exactly where we had intended. A moot point, but gratifying.

Then, G-Man in the lead, we hustled down the bouldery line as rapidly as we dared. The rest of the crew was already at the road, climbing into National Guard Humvees. I considered abandoning the saw, but didn't. Mark had the ax, but jettisoned his swamper pack. We were the last to clamber aboard the trucks, and our crewmates were hooting and hollering at the spectacular fire show. In five minutes we were a half mile down the road, parked in a wide safety zone of bare ground (with a dozer making it yet wider), watching Slide Ridge engulfed in flame.

The next day we were sent back to extinguish spot fires, and on the way up the ridge we paused at The Stump. The wedges were still there, though one had partially melted and flowed down the bark. The swamper pack was vaporized. Among other items, it contained a two-gallon plastic jug of mixed gasoline. We found a blackened scrench and two metal buckles off the straps. I have one before me as I write, a souvenir of conflagration. Mark took home the melted wedge.

So on Day 8, as I passed The Stump, the trenchant recollection of its creation magnified the force of the sundown moment. In such fashion do memories cluster and mingle, engineering a mind, remodeling a life. A few minutes later when we reached the road, and I eased the chain saw off my shoulder, I was not precisely the same entity I had been at the crest of the ridge. I owned an extra veneer of "in-sight," of affirmative innuendo that will help guide the rest of my pilgrimage on this planet, ushering decisions into the church of mind as a phylactery showcases prayer.

A young National Guard sergeant, one of the drivers sent to pick us up, called out, "Hey, man, how was your day?" — an innocuous pleasantry, and any reply would've sufficed, but I was briefly confused. Day? What day?

In my energized state of consciousness his question was received at full face value, each word resounding like a thump of Mark's ax: HOW-WAS-YOUR-DAY? At that instant, the day — as in the previous twelve hours — did not exist. My mind was harnessed to the sundown hike, and *it* was "my day," my eon. If I had the power I might never have reached the road, but rather kept on descending the ridge forever, immersed in perception and memory, weaving entire lifetimes out of sunlight and woodsmoke, braiding thoughts and images into salvation.

.   .   .   .

"Was it hot up there?" the kid asked, open-faced, cheery.

My cognition spiraled to the dust, a spell broken, *the moment* ended. I was back in "real" time, and it was a rough and monotonous two-hour ride back to camp.

"Yeah, Sarge. It was hot."

⑤ The Guts
of God

.

.

.

.

.

.

.

.

.

.

.

I bit my arm, I sucked the blood. . . .
COLERIDGE, The Rime of the Ancient Mariner

"Tonight," Loki assured me, "would be an ideal time to die."

He's a hopeless liar, and merely a fleeting voice in my head, but in the wake of that stunning passage of the autumnal equinox, I agreed. In principle. Mercury and Jupiter had gleamed briefly on the orange stage of dusk, setting forty-five minutes behind the sun. The diurnal solar death was gilded with the aroma of late September. It would be natural to join the dying, be eaten by the earth, digested by trees — in the sheen of waxing starlight.

But I realize it may not have been Loki after all. I suspect it was only the music of his two syllables, a pleasing sound that seemed to honor the pair of twilight planets. Nevertheless there was a voice, or perhaps an echo; a manifestation. Of *manitou*? Of *wakanda* or *ntum*? Maybe *brahman* or *tao*? Should I just go with *magick*? Whatever; all pretty much the same.

Or was Loki completely in-house—a biochemical/electrical snap in the roiling cranial juice of a self-conscious primate? Prelate? Curate?

This thought retrieved from memory the ominous image of Monsignor Schiffer, now decades in his grave, and unrecalled for years. How delightful that the ornery old priest should be summoned by Loki. I see them both in dark robes. I see them as shapeshifters—Loki into a fox or hag, Monsignor Schiffer from his black cassock into the white, gold, and purple vestments that evoked Latin liturgy and transubstantiation, the sacred cannibalism of Christ.

I remembered that at age six I met ghosts—three of them—with stark, chalky faces, and draped in black shrouds. As they bent over other frightened children, cowls slipped from their shoulders and appeared to smother the kids in folds of darkness. I froze in the doorway, clutching my mother's hand.

"Ghosts!" I cried. Mom laughed and said they were nuns, "the sisters." Oh? I never liked them. I feared the nuns, and they feared Monsignor Schiffer—I could see that. Did the Monsignor fear the bishop? The Pope? Or only God? In any case, the fear trickled down.

Twenty years later, on a dayshift at the plant, old Palona told me that Monsignor Schiffer had pockets sewn into his robes—for money—that he had died rich. I didn't believe it, exactly, but the tale meshed into the weave of the minor legend the Monsignor became—priestly to a vengeful fault, glaring from the high pulpit like a gargoyle transmutated from stone. "He is *so* mean," my mother once said.

Palona knew I had a degree in theology, and we joked about launching a ministry, a revenue-raising venture to deliver us from the numbing routine of the plant.

. . . .

The Snow Lotus

"You preach," he growled in his nicotine rasp, "and I follow; collect the money, have overcoat full of pockets . . . like Schiffer!" He laughed and shook the stub of a severed forefinger in my face. "If I had ejacation, I be dangerous!" No lie.

Monsignor Schiffer had an education in "the mysteries." Knowledge is power, said Francis Bacon. Priesthoods of all persuasions have clung to this axiom through ages light and dark. Thus:

Hierarchy: from Greek *hieros*—sacred, holy; *hiero-arch*—holy ruler, high priest; so *hierarchy*—"a system of church government by priests or other clergy in graded ranks." Perhaps like *all* government, as our dictionaries allow today? "If there were no priests," wrote Thomas Jefferson, "there would be no infidels."

If Monsignor Schiffer had heard about me hearing Loki, I would probably have been christened infidel—a ripe solfatara of the underworld, a wiggling helminth in the guts of God. Enema time.

In 1964 the hierarchy invited me to join the club, to retreat to a seminary, but I declined. I eventually turned apostate, and via an agonizing personal Reformation, temporarily evolved into a Protestant. I recall that I sank to my knees beside my desk, upon which lay an open Bible and several fundamentalist tracts, and in fervent miserere consciously accepted Jesus Christ as my personal savior—was later "buried in baptism" through full immersion in a cattle trough, then rose from emblematic death.

It's now January 1994, two weeks after the winter solstice and the holiday season. I loathe Christmas—Salad Shooters and all. Jesus of Nazareth was probably born in late September or early October; learned that at the hardcore Bible college where I got my unaccredited B.A. in Judeo-Christian theology. I was going to be a minister, but was "disfellowshipped" for heresy.

This year some friends gathered for a winter solstice party. We stood around a crackling bonfire in the snow and

.   .   .   .

scribbled our troubles on pieces of notepaper, flinging them into the flames in a symbolic act of release and hope. On a frozen lakeshore beneath a haloed moon, I recited Robert Graves's translation of *The Song of Amergin*: "I am a stag of seven tines. . . ." — ancient Celtic stuff; mythopoetic language; lyrical and beguiling, like an elfin song from *The Lord of the Rings*.

Which reminds me that recently one of our acquaintances who works at a state camp for juvenile delinquents regaled us with a disturbing report. Some out-of-towner billed as an "expert" apprised the boys and the staff of the signs and dangers of satanism. One should be suspicious, the expert said, of people who celebrate the solstices, and also of people who read the works of J. R. R. Tolkien — that professor wrote about demonism!

Our friend was disgusted. It's an old dilemma of etiquette: when confronted with outrageous idiocy, is it more polite to laugh or to weep? And taxpayer dollars were spent on this lecture. Pam mentioned one good thing. If those bad boys have not yet experienced the joys of Middle Earth, they'll probably track down Tolkien's evil books at the earliest opportunity, thus stumbling into some uplifting reading. I hope they won't be disappointed by the goodness.

We'd do better, I think, if experts preached against Beavis and Butthead, or the wretched excess of an American Christmas — hell of a lot more potentially destructive than most of what modern Puritans label "satanism." But it's evident that the intellectual shade of Tomás de Torquemada, inquisitor-general and confessor to Isabella, still thrives beneath the orris shell of darkened hearts. Only his body decomposed in 1498, along with the two thousand humans tortured and executed for heresy. If Tolkien (who was a fervent Christian) and winter solstice observers are the spawn of devils, will we soon be igniting books and witches again? (Feminists — of either sex — may suffice.)

.   .   .   .

The Snow Lotus

Yesterday I heard a New Age entrepreneur on public radio. This guy hires out as a guide for vision questers, and apparently enjoys a thriving trade.

Wait a minute.

Why do people pay someone to help them accomplish something they can only do themselves? It reminded me of the classic definition of a consultant: a person who uses your watch to tell you what time it is. Hey, if you need to embark on a vision quest, then just go. It's absurd for another to tell you *where*. Need to fast for three days and three nights? Just do it. Suffering is free; visions are in the public domain. It was the apostle Paul, fabricator of Christianity and voyager to the third heaven, who is credited with writing: "Work out your own salvation with fear and trembling."

Alas, many will not. As Palona knew, there's money to be made in the trafficking of redemption. We're a modern consumer society. Why should contemporary religion differ from any other commodity? If you don't grow your own food—your very lifeblood—then why should you nurture your own spiritual salvation? There may be a connection between self-reliance and self-respect, with gardening as a metaphor. I've received mail-order catalogs that will accept VISA or MasterCard payment in exchange for enlightenment. Besides, if you plunge too deeply into the forest alone, you may wind up like Conrad's Kurtz, screaming into the night, "The horror! The horror!" Can't have that now, can we? Smacks of demonism.

Then this morning a friend phones to tell me to turn on the television. We've got a major media event, best programming since the Gulf War—the latest Los Angeles earthquake. I tune in and see fire, flooding, bloodied faces, shattered buildings, shattered lives. One glib and breathless TV reporter actually employs the word "apocalyptic," though what I view on the screen pales before the fearful catastrophes of the Book of Revelation. Nevertheless, from my experience as a fundamentalist apologist and glad

.   .   .   .

chortler of Jehovah's holocaust, I know that this earthquake is grist for the preachers' and prophets' mill, that the airwaves and churches will resound with passages read from Matthew 24 and Revelation 6—many intoned with a mien of cautious glee.

The biosphere is, after all, a hateful region, and the sooner Christ returns on his epochal search-and-destroy mission—some might say, pacification program—the sooner we can all be ruled by an omnipotent theocracy. Didn't we try that in the Middle Ages? In the Dark Ages?

Others wait for E. T.

I watch the California images for a few minutes, until the anchor is talking in circles and the same video feeds cycle and recycle to the point of inevitable banality. Yes, tough times for the Angelenos. But I've been a firefighter for thirteen years, have labored at the scene of tragedy and ruin. On the televised faces I recognize the pain, shock, sorrow, and confusion; but I also note the exhilaration and curious joy. I know how that feels. Nothing like a glimpse of death to stir the juices of life. I feel bad for the citizens of L.A., but I also feel jealous. I know that despite the laments they are spouting into seemingly ubiquitous microphones, many will recall this tribulation with fond nostalgia, will never cease speaking of it to the end of their days.

But today I also note that Alice, our eighteen-year-old cat, is probably dying. It was minus forty degrees Fahrenheit this morning, and the balmiest it got in yesterday afternoon's slanted sunshine was minus eighteen. The National Weather Service calls this front a "Siberian payload," a bitter dome of cold air from the old Gulag. It's not directly killing Alice; she lives in the house. But I always figured she'd die in winter—in the midst of one of her long dormant stretches by the woodstove, so still and quiet she could've been a stuffed toy. We joked that when she did pass away, we could take her to a taxidermist, then lay the product on the rug by the stove. In winter, at least, we'd never know the difference.

.   .   .   .

The Snow Lotus

But that's not funny anymore. It turns out that the two puddles of flavescent feline vomit that I cleaned up three days ago were a harbinger. She won't eat. She responds to affection and offers no indication of being in pain, but she's gradually fading away. I gently stroked her ancient neck a few minutes ago, and tears filled my eyes. But unless there's pain, I won't take her to the veterinarian for the fatal injection. The trip to town and the heavily scented, hurt-rich cosmos of the vet's office have always traumatized her, evoking piteous cries and trembling. It would be cruel to subject her to that at the end. It's going to be hard. This lovable little creature has shared our lives, our house, the foot of our bed, since Jerry Ford was president.

I understand, of course, that the demise of this housecat is a minuscule event in the overall global scheme, and some will consider it ludicrous that I even mention it in the context of Los Angeles (not to mention Sarajevo or Mogadishu). But right now it's the only death I've got.

Loki, I suspect, is amused; but I haven't actually heard.

.   .   .   .

৩ Later

.
.
.
.
.
.
.
.
.
.
.

Four lightnings zigzag from me, strike and return.
Navaho Chant

We figured out later that at the precise moment Pam was
in the house talking about Alice, I was crushing her with
the left rear wheel of my pickup truck. Pam was telling
her colleague Maggie that we had to be careful when Alice,
our eighteen-year-old cat, was outside, because she was
nonchalant about vehicles and slow to avoid them. We
had to deposit her on the cedar rail fence—a favorite claw-
sharpener—as a distraction, before we could exit the garage.

That night I was off to fetch a pizza at Bimbo's, and as I
opened the back door Alice slipped out with me. I was un-
concerned. Since it was dark I knew she would pause on the

porch while her eyes adjusted to the gloom. I would be down the road before she hit the sidewalk.

I later recreated the events and determined it required only twenty-six seconds to walk to the truck, get in, start it, and engage the transmission. Unaccountably, Alice was already behind the vehicle, probably lying on the gravel and dusting herself with dirt as she was fond of doing.

I backed out of the garage, swung to the right, then turned down the driveway. I felt a spongy jolt—as if I'd run over a stick or an anthill. At that moment my mind split in two. A layer of awareness just below the level of everyday consciousness knew exactly what that jolt signified. The top layer of mind—centered behind my eyes and focused beyond the windshield—refused to accept the truth for a full three seconds. The truck rolled another twenty-five to thirty feet before the layers were reunited.

Alice! I slammed on the brakes and jammed the stick into reverse. My chest felt numb.

Alice's fur was mostly white, and she was clearly visible in the harsh glare of the backup lights. As I approached she raised her head, looked directly at the truck, and uttered a final cry. It was a surprisingly loud meow, the most plaintive and pitiful sound I've ever heard from an animal, and it ripped through the numbness of my chest. It occurred to me later that she might have thought I was bearing down to hit her again. Did that cry mean "Why?" Why are *you* killing *me*?

I don't even recall getting out of the truck. I knelt by her side and cradled my hands around her head and neck. Surprisingly, there was no gore. She convulsed twice and was dead.

I suppressed a sob. I couldn't weep now. We had company and I was responsible for dinner. Pam and Maggie were basking in the afterglow of a pleasant day spent on the lake. They'd fished in the Women's Walleye Invitational, and Maggie—on her first contest outing, and guided by Pam— had won top prize. I was reluctant to shatter that trium-

.   .   .   .

phant mood just yet, and couldn't visualize breaking down in front of a guest. I gently lifted Alice as if she still lived, and laid her in the back of the old Chevy pickup parked at the edge of the yard.

The next two hours were an eon. After I brought the pizza, Pam and Maggie chatted until past midnight. I attempted to participate, pretending nothing was amiss, but it was torture to watch Pam so cheerful and bright, knowing that I must inevitably admit to Alice's slaughter. Pam loved her deeply. "Watch out for her," she had reminded me, as Alice and I went out the door. Eighteen years! I could barely recall our life without that cat.

Finally, all three of us were yawning—mine more of a show to encourage the other two—and while Pam was showing Maggie to the extra bedroom above the garage, I hustled out to the Chevy and eased Alice into a small cardboard box. When Pam returned to the house, I was sitting on the sofa with the box on my knees, tears dripping from my chin. Pam froze, and paled. "What's wrong!" she cried. I blurted my confession and tipped the box. She wailed, and in a moment we were weeping together, the box nestled between us as we lovingly stroked Alice's fur. Her glazed eyes were still open, and I tried to close them, but it was too late.

In a prelude to *The Biophilia Hypothesis,* Scott McVay wrote: "Through work funded by the Dodge Foundation at the Animal Medical Center by Susan Cohar, we know that the grief experience in the loss of a beloved pet can be as acute and lengthy as that felt after the death of a dear friend or mate." Pam and I can vouch for that. It was 1:00 A.M., so I placed the box on the cool basement slab, and we lay in bed and cried some more.

In early morning, before we woke Maggie, I dug a grave at the edge of the woods near the garden. In summer, Alice had liked to sleep in the dappled shade between the corn rows. We laid the box beside the hole and petted her for the last time. "She's cold," Pam whispered, and handed me a dish towel she'd brought from the house. "Tuck this around her."

I did, then lowered the box to the bottom of the grave. Pam didn't stay to watch the dirt go in. Around noon I resisted an impulse to dig Alice up and scratch behind her ears.

That evening a thunderstorm rumbled in from the west, and through the screens we felt the chill of the front and heard a wave of rain advance across the forest. It whipped down in sheets. I was thinking of our cat out there in the ground when Pam said, "Poor Alice." Tears seeped again.

A week later I had a vivid dream. Alice, ever the stubborn grimalkin, rose from the dead, crawling warm and intact—but pissed—from the grave. I witnessed it from the corn rows, and rushed over to scoop her up and hurry into the house where Pam was stitching a quilt. In the ambience of the dream, Pam was pleased but not surprised. She glibly supplied an acronym for feline resurrection—which I unfortunately did not recall when I awoke—having just read about the phenomenon in some magazine.

That night we discussed the dream, Alice, and our grief. The talk drifted to the prospect of our own deaths, and speculation about an afterlife. Ever the manager and pragmatist, Pam said it seemed "inefficient" that our complex, energy- and labor-intensive earthly lives would be the sum of our existence—"an awful lot of trouble just to die forever."

Several years ago, when we were both fervent fundamentalist Christians, our beliefs had been congruent and firm: all humans who had ever lived would eventually rise from the dead and be judged by God. Most would attain eternal life, and a relative few of the irredeemable evil ones would be destroyed forever in the Lake of Fire. (To its credit our sect rejected the vengeful notion of eternal torment in Hell.) There was a measure of comfort in this dogma, but it was just that. *Dogma*: "a doctrine or body of doctrines formally and authoritatively affirmed." The key word is *authoritatively*, and the root of that authority for us was the acceptance of the Bible as the genuine voice of God. I intensively studied that volume for two decades and concluded that while portions of it are wonderful and useful, and certainly to be read, it was not created and transmitted by a deity, but by fellow humans. That being the case, what made *them* more authoritative than me concerning questions of life, death, and eternity?

I'm reminded of a cartoon strip by Jeff MacNelly. Shoe is complaining that he can't get his computer to work. Cosmo suggests: "Try opening that side panel. Now grab a bunch of stuff in there and jiggle it." Shoe thinks that's ridiculous and orders Cosmo to call The Computer Repair Wizard. This individual, dressed in a peaked cap and robe and brandishing a magic wand, duly appears and fixes the computer. "What did he do?" Shoe asks. "He opened this side panel," Cosmo replies, "grabbed this bunch of stuff and jiggled it around." Chomping on his omnipresent cigar, Shoe snaps, "Well then, what makes him any smarter than *you* or *me*?" Cosmo holds up a piece of paper: "This bill for $135."

Sometimes we're all experts; or at least as expert as we're inclined to be. I've been passionately interested in religion for most of my life. Pam, and several other intelligent and perceptive people I know, have not. This causes me to chuckle and shake my head at times, because for the past twenty-eight years my theological research has verged on the professional in both scope and depth. Examinations of the Judeo-Christian canon — accompanied by much prayer and fasting in a more zealous period — led me into a study of Hebrew and Greek, and sometimes lapped over into the esoteric, as in "beyond the understanding or knowledge of most people; recondite; abstruse." To a lesser degree I also delved into Islam and Buddhism, and for the past decade have also focused on much of the New Age movement. It has been a serious, energetic quest, fraught with intellectual and emotional challenges and hardships, but I chuckle because so far, when all is said and done, I have arrived at more or less the same position some of my friends and acquaintances have held since they were in high school: agnosticism. That is, I simply don't profess to know THE TRUTH, nor maintain a faith in any particular body of doctrine. (I am not an athe-

.   .   .   .

ist. Atheism is simply another dogma that tends to encourage intolerance and narrow-mindedness.)

Most of the time even fans of religion are zeroed in on the routine of daily life more than on theological speculations. But death and other traumas of existence can initiate a resurgence of old doubts, old hopes, and more questions. Yes, Alice was "only" an animal, but there was fire in her eyes, the vital spark of sentience that always seems so potent and durable until it winks out. Her demise carried weight because (1) after nearly two decades of nurturing *I* had carelessly killed her, and (2) we were more intimately involved with the mechanics of corpse and grave than we would have been with a "normal" human death in modern America. *My* hands dug the hole, caressed the body, covered it up. "Alice is dead" was sharp, in-your-face reality, with little leeway for denial.

Our old fundamentalist faith wouldn't have offered much comfort in this case—we didn't believe that animals could earn a haven in the next life. The prophesied theodicy was for humans exclusively, and thus a secret disappointment to many of the faithful, who harbored a closer kinship with Rover or Muffin than with some of their so-called brethren.

And certainly I can claim little in the way of psychic salve for my agnosticism. If it's consolation you crave, then it would be wise to embrace somebody's dogma. There is no shortage of selection, and it's a buyer's market. And realize that most of the available Judeo-Christian offerings consider the concept of animal salvation to be a sort of metaphysical liqueur—a syrupy roborant to ease the pangs of loss. Even many believers think it's OK to tell the kids that puppies go to heaven, a harmless lie in the same league with Santa Claus and the Easter Bunny. And who knows, when justice is considered perhaps Mark Twain hit on the formula when he wrote: "Heaven goes by favor. If it went by merit, you would stay out and your dog would go in."

The discussion Pam and I had about death and its aftermath arrived at no firm conclusion, which is, of course, a routine result for an agnostic. But after a few days of acute melancholy, when all colors seemed faded, all sounds sad, I felt the grief begin to lighten like evening shadows in rising moonlight. I was at a nearby state park for an early afternoon swim, splashing from the lake onto the beach, when I gazed out over the water. The high June sunshine was reflected in a thousand sparkles on the ripples, and my spirit bobbed. Thinking of Alice felt warm instead of cold. I smiled. If I were superstitious I might have decided it was that moment when Alice's soul wafted from her clammy grave to the empyrean reaches of a feline happy hunting ground.

But no, it was merely the character of the day. I had received the proof pages for my latest book; I had worked in our garden and the season appeared promising; I was paid fifty bucks for the old Chevy and was glad to be rid of the rusting hulk; Pam and I had taken a pleasant stroll around Pickerel Lake. These affirmative events helped, but they hadn't explicitly caused the grief to ameliorate. Along with cheerful sunlight on water they were a trigger for the main thing:

Another day was passing, the arrow of time still zinged. It was *later*, simply later.

·   ·   ·   ·   ·   ·   ·   ·   ·   ·   ·   ·   ·   ·

⑤ The Awesome Triple-L

One may not reach the dawn
save by the path of the night.
KAHLIL GIBRAN

I wrote a novel once, worked at it off-and-on for nine years.
I finished it three times, with each incarnation longer and
more complex than the last. A New York literary agent
dubbed it "original," but I didn't let that go to my head. I
knew she was employing *original* as a gentle euphemism
for *weird*. As evidence, I only need mention that one of my
chief characters was a precocious German shepherd named
Francis Bacon, Mr. Bacon for short. Nevertheless, I aggres-
sively marketed the manuscript myself for a while, until I
finally recognized it was mostly crap.

How many hours I sunk into that novel I can only guess, but the time wasn't wasted. Not only did the effort help me learn my craft, it also disclosed the purpose of life. That is, the purpose was revealed to me by one of the characters. You may imagine my surprise when this guy I had named Rocky Bartizan (who hung out with Mr. Bacon) glibly and dramatically—via a game of charades—outlined the three goals of human life, a program he called The Great & Fabulous, Awesome & Vaunted Triple-L.

I've read of authors who claimed their characters somehow assumed lives of their own, and to one degree or another controlled the flow of the story. The writer had no idea how the plot was going to twist and turn, and he or she became as much curious as creative—what *were* those crazy characters going to say or do next? I assumed this was authorial hyperbole, but Benjamin Disraeli, an accomplished novelist as well as notable nineteenth-century British statesman, said, "Whenever I want to read a novel I write one." And H. L. Mencken wrote: "There is in writing the constant joy of sudden discovery; of happy accident."

Well, I don't know about *constant* joy, but I admit that once I was immersed in the writing of a novel, I was occasionally stunned by what the characters—without obvious, conscious effort on my part—would produce. I'll briefly allow Rocky Bartizan (Bart, for short) to speak for himself:

> Mr. Bacon rose to sniff at his face and Bart laughed. He vaulted to his feet and cupped his hands around his mouth. "Yes sir! You stepped right up. Your one thin dime has bought you the magnificent Triple-L: To love! To learn! To laugh! Voila, the purpose of human existence. Thank you, sir. Now please move along to the bearded lady. Next!" He doffed his baseball cap, bowed, and chuckled.
>
> "That's it?" I asked, my voice tinged with sarcasm. "To love, to learn, and to laugh?"
>
> "Hey! What do you want? Some cryptic formula? Some arcane alchemical prescription? The big secret is

.   .   .   .

that there is no big secret. Love, learn, and laugh until you die. The next life, if there is one, will take care of itself if you're faithful to the great Triple-L here and now." He clasped his hands and rolled his eyes toward heaven. "Rocky Bartizan has spoken!"

Indeed. That passage turned out to be on page 128 of a 130-page manuscript; not much point in keeping on after that. I've always blamed Bart for the relatively short length of that novel. Anyway, I bought his program: to love, to learn, and to laugh is the purpose of life. But devising reasons to live is easy. After all, the Triple-L emerged from a guy who was, in the strictest sense, never even alive. (But try and tell that to Mr. Bacon.) The hard part, dear reader, is to keep on loving, learning, and laughing when life is such a bitch. I need not elaborate on its tragedies—large and small, earthshaking and routine—of them you are acutely aware. So I think Bart was saying that the key is to do what you know, despite whatever. If the Triple-L doesn't seem convincing and potent to you, then seek another route. (Bart will not be offended; he is brash, but essentially humble.)

It is the *route*, after all, that's most critical—the *journey* matters more than the destination. That's why I'm a creature and cruiser of the night—on foot, on skis, and via canoe. Daylight is fine, but it's often too bright. Revelation lies in turning your back to the sun and studying the shadows it casts. The night itself is a cosmic shadow, one half of the earth turned away from the sun. Peering into the night, into the shadows, is an exercise similar to writing a novel, a method for rallying with "the constant joy of sudden discovery."

André Malraux, novelist and critic (and fighter pilot during the Spanish Civil War), wrote, "The human mind invents its Puss in Boots and its coaches that change into pumpkins at midnight, because neither the believer nor the atheist is completely satisfied with appearances."

. . . .

So I plumb the night for the same reason I romp with words: to attempt a transcendence of appearances.

On the night of November 8, 1994, I walked down the leaf-cushioned path to Secret Lake, and onto the frosty bog. I have negotiated that path at least four thousand times in darkness, and I fathom it by feel. I take no flashlight or head-lamp because they pollute night vision. In fact, when my pupils are not yet fully dark-adapted, it is easier to follow the path if I close my eyes and shut out all visual cues, sub-mitting to the practiced touch of feet on the trail and finger-tips on branches. The path has a discernible "flow"; it matches the terrain as if it belongs—like a red pine in sandy soil or a downy woodpecker on an aspen snag. Maybe that's because the path was originally fashioned by deer, and later adopted by one of our dogs, who made a daily trip to the lake on summer afternoons. Hooves and paws established the route, and though my boots have scuffed it a little wider and deeper, the deer still use it.

It was just after 6:00 P.M., but the sun had set several minutes before five o'clock, and I liked that. I think of winter less as a season of snow and ice than as a season of starlight and moonshadow. When I reached the water's edge I noted that Arcturus was low in the west, glinting amid the faintest smear of latent twilight. The prominent summer constellations—Lyra, Aquila, Cygnus—were displaying their circumpolar spin, canting to the north away from the zenith. In the east, the Pleiades had just cleared the forest canopy.

Other than an appreciation of fresh nightfall, my mis-sion was to spot the space shuttle *Atlantis*. It was supposed to swing into view at 6:10 for this latitude, and it did. I spotted the craft near Arcturus. A swift white sparkle that was a bit brighter than Polaris, it was tracking in a shallow arc from northwest to southeast. When I focused on the fact that this speck of light was about 250 miles away, its mo-tion was astonishing. I happen to know that a shuttle's or-bital velocity is roughly 16,000 miles per hour, or four-and-

· · · · · · · · · · · · · ·

The Snow Lotus

one-half miles every second, the equivalent of a jaunt from Minneapolis to the Ontario border in a minute. Of course I have no way of directly measuring these values; the numbers are rote knowledge. From the shore of Secret Lake, the magnificent machine *Atlantis* looked like a renegade star, a shocking violation of the serene celestial order, like a comet or a meteor.

I tried to visualize the shuttle, inside and out, as I recalled it from numerous photographic and video images, and I could picture the familiar stub-winged ship easily. But I had a tough time projecting the six-person crew out to that point of light. *There were humans in the night sky.* I'd even read a couple of their names—McMonagle, Ochoa—in a newspaper story. Never heard of them. Unlike the missions of Mercury and Gemini, when each launch was a routine-interrupting, national spectacle, people orbiting the earth in space vehicles now seems unremarkable. Astronauts are no longer celebrated household names, but a guild of nearly anonymous technicians. The last truly famous ones were those killed on the *Challenger*. The newspaper had mentioned that the *Atlantis* crew was keeping "a rather low profile," but as I watched the reflection of the shuttle in the calm black water of Secret Lake, I knew that having humans in the the sky *is* remarkable. I was not satisfied with appearances, nor with Puss in Boots and pumpkins.

There are several versions of the fairy tale Puss in Boots, but the basic plot is this: A working class lad is left only a cat for his inheritance (his two older brothers get the good stuff), and he despairs, figuring he might skin the animal and at least make a cap. He's convinced that he'll soon be so poor that starvation will loom. But the cat is special, and urges the youth to provide it with boots and a large drawstring bag, and thus equipped the cat will earn a good living for them both. By means of several clever tricks, Puss persuades the king that his master is a rich nobleman called the Marquis de Carabas. For example, as the finale to his scheme, Puss needs to provide the "Marquis" with a castle

.   .   .   .

to impress the king. He appears at the fine palace of a shapeshifting ogre and brazenly challenges the monster by pretending to doubt its power. In response, the ogre proudly transforms itself into a lion. Puss professes to be only moderately amused, and says, "Marvelous, but can you become something tiny? Surely it is only rumor that you can change into a mouse." The ogre roars that it can indeed, and becomes a mouse. Puss instantly pounces, gobbling it up, and his master takes over the palace. The boy eventually marries the princess and ends up wealthy and aristocratic, in fact.

When I reread the tale, it struck me as a synopsis of the American Dream. True, we would emphasize hard work rather than deceit, but Puss in Boots does demonstrate the resourcefulness and courage that popular opinion ascribes to successful entrepreneurs.

I happen to recall my first exposure to the term *American Dream*. It was a certain cover illustration on a scholastic magazine that all students received each week in our grade school. A ship (circa World War I), decks crowded with European immigrants, is sailing into New York. In the background is the Statue of Liberty. The headline for the cover story was: "What Is the American Dream?" It slowly dawned on me as I read the article that both sets of my grandparents had arrived in the United States in exactly that manner only a few decades before. Why did they come? It's rare that anyone does anything for a single reason, but basically they came for work. However, not just for something to do—they sought jobs that would engender *prosperity*, a degree of material success that seemed far-fetched or impossible in "the old country." It's true that they, and millions of others, ended up not only with prosperity but also with an open society and political freedom, but mainly it was the money. The fundamental nature of the American Dream is summed up in the one-line self-description of the *Wall Street Journal*: "The daily diary of the American dream." It's tempting to embellish the concept with paeans to opportunity, industry, and equality, but at root the

Dream is encapsulated as: every man a rich man, or at least potentially rich.

And to a large extent we've done it—especially compared to the rest of the world, both present and past. Our wealth is unprecedented. Americans constitute about 5 percent of the world's population, and utilize/consume about 30 percent of the world's resources, including a full quarter of the fossil fuels burned each year. Eighty-nine percent of American households own one or *more* automobiles. The average American child enjoys $230 per year in pocket money, which exceeds the entire annual income of at least a half-billion of the world's poorest inhabitants. We watch TV commercials showing housecats munching expensive entrées from glass stemware, while other ads urge us to spend thousands of dollars of disposable income on frivolous and destructive toys like ATVs and jet skis. Our general affluence has reached such giddy heights that we can apparently afford to invest 2,200 calories of energy into the production of a diet soft drink that provides only one calorie of food energy. And of course we can spend billions of dollars to install humans in the night sky.

Atlantis is the culmination of the American Dream. Only massive quantities of wealth can sustain a space program, and the ultimate goal is to ship immigrants out into the rest of the solar system and beyond—the new and final frontier. They shall go looking for work. It is heady, inspiring stuff—a lunar colony with mines, observatories, and a spaceport; perhaps a "terraformed" Mars that could support billions of people; an outpost on Ganymede with Jupiter spanning its horizon; someday starships pushing out into the vastness of the galaxy. In the context of how the human mind perceives time and space, there is no practical limit—certainly not the sky. I remember being on my paper route when I was in junior high school, and one winter evening under a streetlamp on 4th Avenue North, I used a stick to inscribe my favorite epigram into a snowbank: "Too low they build, who build beneath the stars." (Edward Young)

.   .   .   .

Nevertheless, even after an adolescence steeped in science fiction novels and space-age dreams, I could not "see" the crew of *Atlantis* from the shore of Secret Lake. During the four or five minutes it required for the speck of light to cross the sky before vanishing into haze on the southeastern horizon, I watched it mainly as a reflection on the water. I saw its image merge with the sphagnum moss before it actually left the firmament.

My eyes lingered on the moss, the lean, mean acidic sphagnum that is gradually colonizing Secret Lake, closing a circle of centuries to transform the open water to bog. It reminded me of another night journey, several years before on the Sioux River. My partner and I were each in our own canoe, laden with gear and bear meat, the result of a long but ultimately successful hunt in the Boundary Waters Canoe Area Wilderness. The late-September weather was uncharacteristically mild, and in a rush to pack out the hard-earned meat before it spoiled, we pushed our canoes into Shell Lake after dark, heading for Upper Pauness and the mouth of the Sioux. The moon was phased between last quarter and new, and would thus rise far too late to help us, but we knew the route well, and starlight was a sufficient guide.

However, even before we portaged into Pauness, a bank of dense clouds swept in from the south, and the night became opaque—shadowless, featureless. On the expansive mirror of the lake there was enough ambient reflection to shepherd us across, but once we breached the river there was only blackness. The prow of my canoe seemed distant, ghostly. Though less than fifty yards behind, my companion and his canoe were invisible. We had about four-and-a-half miles of paddling from the mouth to the final portage, and I realized with a start that it was now possible for us to become lost on this familiar river.

The problem was an ample growth of wild rice that had choked the wide, meandering stream down to a narrow channel—only a few yards across in some stretches. It was like moss encroaching on a bog pond. If we paddled into the

.   .   .   .

The Snow Lotus

thicket of stalks and missed the channel, it would be possible to travel in circles all night or, at best, to struggle through the paddle-fouling rice at a huge cost in time and effort.

So the key was to stroke slowly and quietly, listening. As soon as I heard the faint tick-tick-tick of my prow brushing rice stalks, I would swing the canoe in the opposite direction and try to follow the channel until I heard the telltale ticking on the other side. And thus was I guided upriver by the rice, bumping from one margin of the channel to the other. Though I didn't actually see the river, I have never experienced it so vividly, nor so intimately traced its course. I was like Puss in Boots, overcoming appearances, rising above my station. As a daylight-dependent species, most humans do not often cross over and rise up to trek in the rich realm of the night.

But there are humans in the night sky.

After *Atlantis* disappeared, I stood by the water for several minutes, conjuring up images of the earth from space, trying to imagine the view of the astronauts from high above the middle of the North American continent. I was speculating on the potential of them spotting Secret Lake, when it occurred to me that the astronauts couldn't see it anyway because they were over the night half of the planet, and probably able to watch only the sparkling of artificial light from major population centers, the nocturnal glow of the American Dream—ubiquitous spoor of megawatts and money.

I called to the Reverend and we turned for the house, eyes fully adapted to soothing darkness. A five-day-old moon illuminated the path as well as we needed it to be. Back inside, I stoked the woodstove against the late autumn chill, then switched off the living room lamp and stretched out on the sofa. I gazed out our "widescreen" window at a western sky framed by aspen and fir tops. With the interior of our house as dark as the forest, and my mind wrestling with the character of the cosmos beyond the glass, I decided that I could not "see" the astronauts because I no longer marshaled a fervent faith in their mission. Despite the virtuosity of Asimov, Norton, Heinlein, and dozens of other luminaries of the imagination—not to mention the actual achievements of NASA—I realized that the human foray into space had become a moral problem. Is it right that we expand beyond our home planet before we have come to terms with it? Shall we colonize other worlds without having learned how to properly and sustainably thrive on our own? Will we be consumers not only of fossil fuels and diet soda, but of planets as well? Is the American Dream intended to become the Earthling Dream, to be exported beyond the solar system regardless of merit? Is our lipophilic culture destined to race ATVs across the deserts of Mars? Perhaps we are like Puss in Boots, advancing beyond our means via clever tricks, but fooling only ourselves. How long can 5 percent of the species, awash with wealth and yearning for the heavens, avoid the judgment—right or wrong—of all the humans who yearn only for survival? Maybe forever. Maybe the galaxy *is* the mandate of the American Dream, and Asimov will be celebrated on a par with Galileo (or Moses). Perhaps it is I who have not transcended appearances.

But I keep thinking of the rice—of the tick-tick-tick on the hull of my canoe, and how it, and not the stars, steered me up the river I couldn't see. In both spirit and form, I am closer kin to the rice than I am to the nuclear furnaces of the stars, and I will not share the American Dream if it means I must hope for the consumption of planets. My purpose is not expansion.

My purpose was outlined by Bart—his Great & Fabulous, Awesome & Vaunted Triple-L: to love, to learn, to laugh. And I realize that such may be a luxury, another privilege of the rich. All I can say is that I *do* feel privileged. I will keep traveling by night.

And a few days after I spotted *Atlantis* I read the following news item about the shuttle: "Mission Control, meanwhile, kept an eye on an icicle, four to five feet long and an

.   .   .   .

inch in diameter, hanging from one of *Atlantis'* cargo bay doors. The icicle formed a few days ago when urine and other waste water were being dumped overboard."

There is piss in the night sky.

Do you see what I mean about us being out there?

. . . .

⑤ Ditching the Future

We are bound to the rest of life in our ecology,
our physiology, and our spirit.
E. O. WILSON

When I was thirteen years old, my brother David was seven and a half. Because of that age difference, we weren't buddies. The school system—omnipotent social arbiter—had established us six grades apart. Though most students are analogous by the time of graduation, or at least more alike than different, a span of six grades is treated as a broad social and cultural gulf. As a rule, seventh-graders don't associate with first-graders, and that's certainly the way my friends and I felt in the summer of 1963. There are, of course, other distinctions between puberty-wracked early teens and kids fresh out of kindergarten, but the stilted, age-stratified nature of the schools severely exaggerates the natural contrasts.

On a day over thirty years ago that remains vivid in recollection, my pack of junior high school pals and I "ditched" David. It was axiomatic that he was forbidden entry to our circle, even if our play happened to be age-neutral at a given time—like assembling model planes, playing hide-and-seek, or horsing around on the monkey bars at the park. His earnest young face confronts me across the decades, round and radiant with the innocence of a child not yet betrayed.

He was hovering near my fellow barbarians and I as we lounged on one of the neighborhood porches, mulling over options for a precious July afternoon. David just wanted to be with his big brother. I ordered him to go away. He wouldn't. I yelled at him: "Go home!" No, he wanted to play with us. It is to my credit, I suppose, that I didn't shove or strike him (at least not that time). Instead, my buddies and I decided that if he wouldn't leave us, we'd leave him.

Bunching into a gang, we strode off. David followed. We broke into a run. He ran, and dropped back quickly, his shorter, first-grade-in-the-fall legs not able to match our adolescent strides. But he gained, then held our pace—about fifteen yards behind—as we raced through yards, cut across alleys, vaulted picket fences. I glanced back several times, sure we'd lost him, but he was sprinting his heart out, his expression grim and hurt. I felt ashamed, but kept loping with the pack, too committed to the opinion of my peers to cut my brother any slack. I should have stopped and said, "Hey, David, you're tough, you're OK." I should have called out to my cohort and convinced them that my little brother's determination had earned him a place in our clique, at least for that afternoon. I probably could've swayed them, but I didn't try.

After several minutes of dogged chase, David finally gave up. A final glance revealed him leaning against yet another fence, panting and probably crying. I ran on.

I recalled that scene as I sat down to write about population—that is, the exponential growth of our human species. At root, it's about families—their propagation and process. Leaving David behind on that summer day is linked in my memory with another episode from that era—in February—either the winter before or after.

There was a tremendous accumulation of snow, and our father had molded a huge pile from the tons shoveled off the driveway. He smoothed one side and sprinkled it with water to create an icy slide, and I was perched on top, clutching a piece of cardboard I was using as a makeshift toboggan. It was almost dark under a lowering overcast, and I was staring at the house. There was a light on in the kitchen and the windowpane was an orange glow in the winter gloom. I had just stifled a sob, and was blinking to deny tears passage to my cheeks. Some run-of-the-mill family calamity had driven me outdoors, and at that moment I resolved—for no intellectual reason I can recall—to never be a father. Why that moment, or any other particular moment, remains clear through the decades is often a mystery. But I am surprised and bemused to realize that it was a resolution I was destined to keep. For better and for worse I opted out of a personal familial response to the world, and forswore an element of basic biology that seems all-important to many.

As years passed I articulated a rationale for my sudden decision on the snow pile. In 1968, *The Population Bomb* by Paul Erlich appeared, and though I never read it, the message and its main supporting points became more or less common knowledge. On the cover was the warning "Population Control or Race to Oblivion," and a promotional blurb condensed the message: "Overpopulation is now the dominant problem in all our personal, national, and international planning." I would, I thought, avoid contributing to the problem.

The specter of human self-destruction via runaway reproduction played into the prophetic scheme of a fundamentalist Christian sect that attracted me as a member for a few years during my college career, and since the flock passionately believed that the second advent of Christ was imminent, it made little practical sense to develop any long-term worldly arrangements—especially planning for a family.

But family planning was on the minds of many. In July of 1969, President Richard Nixon delivered a "Special Message to the U.S. Congress on Problems of Population Growth." He said, in part:

> In 1917 the total number of Americans passed 100 million, after three full centuries of steady growth. In 1967 . . . the 200 million mark was passed. If the present rate of growth continues . . . by the year 2000, or shortly thereafter, there will be more than 300 million Americans. [There are 260 million now—October 1994—and at the present growth rate we'll top 300 million around 2008.] . . . Where . . . will the next 100 million Americans live? . . . How will we educate and employ such a large number of people? Will our transportation systems move them about as quickly and economically as necessary? How will we provide adequate health care when our population reaches 300 million? Will our political structures have to be reordered, too, when our society grows to such proportions? . . . We should establish as a national goal the provision of adequate family planning services within the next five years to all those who want them but cannot afford them.

Nixon's concern for political structures strikes a disturbing historical chord. As population burgeons, civil rights necessarily erode. Two prominent examples of such erosion stem from fear of crime (and the creation of new trespasses and laws) and worries about the environment.

As more people concentrate in urban areas, the statutory power of the police is enhanced. When the nation was young, rural, and thinly populated, citizens had little thought of gun control, parking violations, curfews, or mandatory licenses to operate a vehicle, own a dog, or fish in public waters. The more people that inhabit a given space, the more regulation is required. Where I live, in the backwoods of northeastern Minnesota, serious crime is not a worry—it's just too rare. That's because our population density is low, a luxury most humans don't enjoy. In 1984, there were thirty-four metropolitan areas in the world with populations in excess of five million, and United Nations demographers projected that by 2025 there will be ninety-three such cities. It's ironic, but the more humanity "civilizes," that is, abandons a rural landscape for an urban one, the greater the threat of chaos. A recent anecdote about metropolitan police power was reported on ABC radio. A traffic cop in Bangkok (a city of more than five million inhabitants, expected to reach fifteen to twenty million by 2025) apparently became thoroughly frustrated by the congestion and gridlock on a particularly hectic thoroughfare. He manipulated the signals so that every light was green simultaneously. As dozens of cars smashed together in the middle of the intersection, the cop was witnessed in their midst—dancing.

How long before the entire system cracks? How much additional state control will it require to keep a society of 300 million Americans (or more) at peace and in order? Already some governors have tapped the resources of the National Guard to aid police officers, and, as I write this, the mayor of Washington, D.C., has asked President Clinton for the same power. How authoritarian will we need to become?

The Chinese might have an answer. So critical is the population problem in China that the central government is attempting to directly regulate the birthrate. Enforced sterilization and abortions are part of the strategy, along with floggings. Repugnant, and "Big Brother" personified, but how do you control one billion humans? What will they eat? Where will they live? How long can the land (which does not expand) support them?

In his Pulitzer Prize–winning book *The Diversity of Life*, professor and researcher Edward O. Wilson presents compelling evidence that the earth is undergoing its sixth great extinction of life forms. The previous five, including the demise of the dinosaurs sixty-five million years ago, resulted from cataclysms that probably involved asteroid/meteorite impacts, widespread volcanism, and general climatic change. But this sixth wave of extinctions is being caused by the accelerated needs and demands of a single species: *Homo sapiens.* The hallmark of the disturbing event, says Wilson, is a loss of biological diversity:

> Human demographic success has brought the world to this crisis of biodiversity. Human beings—mammals of the 50-kilogram weight class and members of a group, the primates, otherwise noted for scarcity—have become a hundred times more numerous than any other land animal of comparable size in the history of life. By every conceivable measure, humanity is ecologically abnormal. Our species appropriates between 20 and 40 percent of the solar energy captured in organic material by land plants. There is no way we can draw upon the resources of the planet to such a degree without drastically reducing the state of most other species.

Hence the environmental concern, and the need to regulate how individuals and communities dispose of waste, how and what they consume, what they do on their own property. For example, we own forty acres of forest land. Although the time is long since past when we might do whatever we pleased on our own turf (open a landfill, for instance), the rules will likely be significantly more stringent soon. In Minnesota there is a push to adopt the "Forest Practices Act." In essence, it means the government (that is, the community at large), would dictate how I managed my forest, and it would not be strictly up to me if and when and how I cut my timber—or not. Intrusive and un-American? A case could be made, but the Act is an implicit recognition of the fact that there are too many of us to allow the helter-skelter private management of a resource as valuable as a forest. What I do with my trees not only affects me and my immediate neighbors, but, multiplied by all the other forties

.   .   .   .

　　　　　　　　　　　　　　　　The Snow Lotus

in the watershed, has a potential impact on thousands of people and, ultimately, on the biosphere itself. Such forestry rules are already law in Sweden, a nation not as densely populated as our own.

A couple of months ago I received a telling missive from the government of Costa Rica. As part of a Rainforest Action Network letter-writing campaign, I'd sent a card to the Costa Rican minister of Natural Resources, Energy, and Mines regarding proposed development in that nation that might have a negative impact on the pristine habitats of the Osa Peninsula.

In reply to my concerns, the minister detailed what environmental safeguards Costa Rica was planning. He also mentioned how much it would cost to acquire the private land that remains in the midst of their parks and reserves, and cagily suggested, "Perhaps your organization might be interested in helping us to solve this particular problem." Between the lines I read: instead of spending so many dollars on postage to criticize our efforts, why don't you rich North Americans put your money where your mouth is and help us purchase these private holdings that endanger the integrity of our reserves?

The last paragraph was more explicit: "Also, we do realize that we all share a common and only world and, in the long run, we all will confront the same fate. As such, I am much concerned of what happens in the industrialized countries where most of the world's pollution and environmental degradation occurs as a direct consequence of ill-planned development. Perhaps, as folklore suggests, we shall not just look at the chaff in other's eye while missing the stick in our own."

Touché.

The "folklore" he mentions (albeit a bit garbled) is a reference to the words of Jesus in the seventh chapter of the Book of Matthew. In that same chapter we read that "by their fruits you shall know them." It's interesting to compare that with verse 28 of the second chapter of Genesis

(New English Bible): "God blessed them [Adam and Eve] and said to them, 'Be fruitful and increase, fill the earth and subdue it, rule over the fish in the sea, the birds of heaven, and every living thing that moves upon the earth.'"

Yes, we've been fruitful, and by those fruits we are now known. There was a time when it made good sense to "increase," when survival hinged on the sheer number of hunters, farmers, mothers, and laborers available to perform the work of life. That time has passed; now it is sheer numbers that threaten our well-being.

Why is it then that Americans continue to multiply? Let's heed, for the moment, the admonition of the Costa Rican resources minister and consider the "stick" in our own eye, noting in fairness that part of the American increase is due to immigration from the minister's region of the world.

There are two basic motives for modern Americans to have children: (1) conformity, and (2) self-indulgence.

Conformity. Some people have kids simply because most couples do, and it is thus the normal course. They eat, they breathe, they copulate; therefore they reproduce. Some people are pressured by family to extend the line. I once asked a college buddy why he wanted to have children. His reply: so he could have grandchildren; unassailable logic.

Self-indulgence. People are incessantly regaled with accounts of the joys and fulfillment of parenthood, and many desire those feelings in their own lives. Many parents view their offspring as a means of transcending death. Producing children is sometimes (perhaps often) seen as a way to save a marriage, "fix" a life, or otherwise improve a situation that may have nothing to do with the advantages of parenthood. Through laziness, ignorance, or apathy (all forms of self-indulgence), many people reproduce by accident. Some consider it their religious and/or patriotic duty to increase the population, and derive personal gratification from accomplishing the mission. (Through antiquated income tax incentives Americans are financially rewarded by their gov-

.   .   .   .

ernment for creating more citizens.) Some see an opportunity to relive their lives through their children, and in that sense the kids are toys—essentially sophisticated pets—to be manipulated and molded for the sake of personal power. Children can foster the illusion of destiny control, and the allure of the "second chance." For some, children appear to be just another consumer item, like a new car or boat—something to flaunt to neighbors and relatives. The decision to have progeny is not often based on rational considerations.

I'm not suggesting that we collectively cease having children, but it's apparent that family planning—intelligent reproduction—has not firmly taken hold in this country. In 1991 our fertility rate was 2.1 (on the rise from 1.8, where it had stabilized for a while), and that guarantees an increasing population without even factoring in the effects of immigration.

In his book *Around the Cragged Hill*, ex-ambassador George F. Kennan, a man with an expansive view of history and public affairs, wrote of

> the optimal balance, depending upon the manner of man's life, between the density of human population and the tolerances of nature. This balance, in the case of the United States, would seem to me to have been surpassed when the American population reached, at a very maximum, two hundred million people, and perhaps a good deal less. . . . And there is a real question as to whether "bigness" in a body politic is not an evil in itself, quite aside from the policies pursued in its name.

I'm satisfied that many of our national and global problems—starvation, environmental degradation, political unrest, crime—have their roots in overpopulation. Erlich was right. Indeed, the slogan of Negative Population Growth, Inc., an organization dedicated to reducing the U.S. population to about 135 million (what it was around 1940) and world population to two billion is: "Any cause is a lost cause without a reduction in population."

.   .   .   .

Consider the moose of Isle Royale. A large, roadless island in Lake Superior, Isle Royale National Park is, in its relative isolation, a metaphor for the earth—there's only so much room. About ninety years ago, moose appeared on the island, probably swimming the fifteen or so miles from the Ontario mainland. With no predators and abundant forage, the moose population exploded, and by the early 1930s the food supply was being consumed faster than it could regenerate. By 1937 the population crashed, decimated by starvation.

In simple terms, that's the potential of our own situation, especially in the developing world. If present rates of global population growth are projected for a few hundred years, we see the planet literally sheathed with people—a teeming, seething mass of human flesh that is expanding into outer space at the speed of light. Obviously that's absurd. Like the moose of Isle Royale, we'll crash long before then. One way or another it's certain that our numbers will eventually decline, the only questions being: How? Will the decline be catastrophic or gradual? And what will be the condition of our earth/island?

The moose population of Isle Royale did recover and stabilize. However, it's interesting to note that stabilization was achieved because, during the especially frigid winter of 1948–1949, an ice bridge formed between the island and Canada, allowing a wolf pack to cross the ice and take up residence. The predators thrived, and population control for the moose was established. Who or what will be *our* "predators"?

So over the years I've found reasons and numbers to support my personal proscription of fatherhood. It was a good decision, and the rationale of not contributing to overpopulation is sincere and sound. But I admit there is also a facet of the decision that makes a virtue of necessity—the "necessity" of plotting a course through life that one feels *compelled* to follow. It's clear that my sudden resolution atop the snow pile at the green age of thirteen or fourteen originated somewhere besides and beyond cold, hard calculation.

. . . .

Perhaps I was intimidated by the awesome responsibility of generating and shaping another human life. As I've joked (half-seriously) to friends, we (Pam decided to share the course) took the easy way out.

There is a reason, I think, that the image of "ditching" David and the epiphany on the sliding mound are so strongly linked in memory. They both speak to the small but powerful actions of childhood, a stage of life utterly dependent on the structure of family. When people have children, it's not so much to create individuals, but households. We reproduce in bunches, and our focus should not be on fewer people per se, but on smaller families, smaller communities, smaller nations. Since we were all nurtured in families of one sort or another, and by definition at an impressionable age, our urge is to extend these groups in numbers and through time. In the pure biological sense, children are born to be parents. But not me.

I had a good childhood, filled with wonder and challenge. Nevertheless, in my mind—at some obscure level—it wasn't good enough to replicate.

Is our contemporary society and world—ripping at the seams with billions of our demanding fellows—good enough to replicate? Wise enough to be worthy of magnification again and again? When I ran from my brother so many years ago, I was following the herd. We all do that at times—it's easy, and sometimes compulsory. But it's vitally important at this late date that we devote more critical attention to that instinct.

And also decrease the herd.

. . . .

Nasty Business

It's dangerous, *I know, and it can hurt a lot.*
Kilgore Trout

I'll call the victim Sulo, and if Neil and I had known his plan, we'd never have invited him into the sauna. I was helping Neil construct a boathouse out of cedar logs a few bright summers ago, and we worked hard at it all day. Neil lit his neighbor's sauna after lunch, and periodically stoked the firebox the rest of the afternoon. We anticipated a relaxing steambath after our labors, and we wanted it hot.

Visitors dropped by shortly before dusk, as we were tying up the project for the day. It was a friends-of-friends situation, and neither Neil nor I knew Sulo. We got acquainted over a few beers, and Neil assured Sulo he was welcome to join us in the sauna.

When the three of us settled in on the top bench, we realized the stove was far too hot. Most of the stovepipe was glowing cherry-red, and Neil figured he'd gotten carried away with the stoking. He cautioned us not to throw water on the rocks, or terrific, scalding steam would drive us to the floor. In a traditional sauna, a woodstove heats a bed of rocks, and water is tossed on the rocks to generate a soothing, cleansing steam. An agreeable bath can be achieved at 125 to 150 degrees, but the temperature in this particular sauna was over 200.

Sulo tipped back his beer bottle, sucked down a long strapping swig, and rhapsodized about saunas past, boasting of how much heat he could endure. Neil and I exchanged nervous glances behind his back. Our aim was restoration, not a vain trial of stamina.

After fifteen minutes of the intense heat, Neil and I needed to cool down outside. We still didn't dare throw water on the baking rocks, and it seemed Sulo was impatient. Maybe he thought he was sharing this purification rite with a couple of overcautious wimps—and non-Scandinavians to boot.

We were out in the bracing evening air for less than a minute when we heard a loud, explosive KA-KOOSH! from inside the sauna, followed by a prolonged, crackling hiss. We shook our heads and grinned. Sulo had let her rip. It sounded like he'd dumped an entire pail of water on the rocks. Clouds of steam puffed out of the soffits and curled up around the eaves.

"It must be like a pressure cooker in there," I said.

Neil nodded, still ruefully shaking his head.

When I eased back inside a few minutes later, Sulo was prostrate on the top bench, breathing heavily. His face was flushed, and he appeared to be in pain.

"You all right?" I asked.

"Yeah," he croaked, and pushed himself up to a sitting

position. He was still clutching his beer bottle. Neither of us knew it yet, but his back was burned; the rush of broiling steam had seared his flesh. The day after next he'd be in the hospital having his back abraded, but this was merely the beginning of sorrows.

It was an inherently hazardous sauna building. The benches were too high and steep, the room too cramped. We were precariously perched directly over the woodstove on slippery, wet surfaces. Mix in a few beers, and disaster loomed. And Sulo's senses had been further numbed by the horrendous blast of steam.

The heat from that burst was lingering over the top bench, so I sat on the next level down. Though the skin on Sulo's back still looked normal, his breathing continued to sound labored, and it dawned on him that he was partially cooked.

"You sure you're OK?" I asked.

"Well . . . maybe I better take a little break."

He took a big one. He raised his red butt off the bench and fell forward. I was horrified. For a wild moment I thought: this dude is dead. As he dropped by me I was certain he was going to land on the stove and rocks and be fried. Instead, he dove six feet onto the concrete floor, impacting with an ugly bellyflop. I heard the beer bottle shatter in his hand, which was sandwiched between the floor and his stomach. Before I could move to stop him, he rolled over in a panicky spasm, and his abused back slid into the side of the woodstove. There was a sizzling hiss, and Sulo moaned. The floor was splattered with blood and glass.

Neil whipped open the door and stopped short when he saw the shards of glass. With bare feet there wasn't much he could do. But Sulo had already struggled to his knees. I heaved a sigh of relief. He was stout, and if he'd been unconscious it would've been a monumental struggle to haul him out.

Sulo stumbled to the door, and I followed as quickly as I could, gingerly tiptoeing through the blood and debris.

.   .   .   .

There was a crimson puddle on the floor, and it looked like we'd dressed out a buck, or maybe prepared the set of a horror movie. We guided Sulo to a large Norway pine just outside the sauna, and propped him against the trunk. Neil grabbed a five-gallon bucket of cold water and poured it over Sulo's back. The skin was black where it had pressed into the stove, but Sulo said the rinse made him feel better.

Back in the sauna's anteroom we helped him dress and inspected his wounds. His stomach and thigh had been slashed by the broken bottle, and we were able to pluck one splinter of glass out of him then and there. He also had a deep laceration at the base of this right thumb. That was oozing the most blood, and we tightly wrapped a washcloth around his hand.

We hustled him back to Neil's, where there happened to be a registered nurse on the premises, and we suggested that Sulo let her examine him. He refused. He knew, he said, how to handle these matters, and would go home now and do it. I suspect he was embarrassed by the incident and just wanted to get the hell out of there. As he stiffly eased into his car, grunting, the nurse urged him to drive directly to the hospital in town.

But he hurried home, and we later learned that upon arrival he bared his scarred, parboiled back, and instructed his wife to pour alcohol over it. His resulting scream of agony was so horrible that she vomited. We've not seen Sulo since, and we don't expect to—at least not at that particular sauna.

We cleaned up the sauna that night, and, considering the carnage, we did a fair job. But Neil returned the next day to find we'd missed a spot. There on the sauna door, where Sulo had apparently leaned for a second on his way out, was a perfectly formed, bloody handprint. It was the moment made visible, an instant symbolically preserved as a graphic cautionary tale. Neil declared that if he owned the sauna he would've left it there—laid a coat of varnish over it—as a dramatic reminder to all comers that there should be no

.   .   .   .

The Snow Lotus

glass bottles in the sauna. Of such simple rules does most of life consist.

Of course a steambather should also watch his footing. If Sulo had thoroughly scouted that fateful step off the top bench, he may not have fallen—or at least his dive may have been more graceful. Perhaps he could have avoided landing on the beer bottle. In a more carefully considered descent, he would have held the bottle away from his body. He also wouldn't have executed that frivolous twist into the side of the stove. Good form always pays.

That reminds me of a certain summer afternoon on the Sturgeon River. Pam and I were in one canoe, and Neil and Mar in another. We were exploring a short stretch new to us—about six river miles—and we expected a lazy, two-hour paddle in the sunshine. Mar was wearing a brand new pair of eyeglasses, and she was merrily raving about how crisp and fresh the summer appeared through those lenses.

But the pleasant riverine promise was only good for about ten minutes. Around the second bend we encountered the first of several nasty logjams. That section of river is slow and meandering, and several years' worth of forest debris had collected at the choke points of the sharper curves. The straighter, faster length of river upstream rises during spring runoff, lifts its accumulation of fallen trees and limbs, and washes it all down to the flats.

Such jams can be deadly. The twisted mass of trunks and branches is a treacherous puzzle. Until you test a given log with your weight, it's often impossible to tell if it's securely jammed and stable, or if it's floating free, poised to roll out from under your feet. It's a birler's version of Russian roulette.

A jam on the Sturgeon can be several yards wide, and if you were to drop through it, the current could easily drag you underneath the floating dam, trapping you below the surface. Of course there's no law that states you must risk traversing a jam. It's almost always an option to pull your canoe up the bank and portage around. But in the flats the banks are steep, muddy, and thick with brush, and it usually seems easier to take your chances on the jam.

So our placid float trip mutated into an arduous challenge. Brief periods of free paddling were bracketed by tangled revetments of deadfalls. Some of them were five or six feet high, and fifteen to twenty feet wide. In most cases Pam and I would ease the canoe up to a log that looked anchored, then one of us would hop out and steady the boat. Using sticks to poke ahead—like testing punky ice—we'd determine a relatively secure path over the jam. Sometimes it helped to drag the canoe along as we reconnoitered, using it as a support and battering ram. It was sweaty, time-consuming labor, and our two-hour jaunt was evolving into five.

As often happens in life—if not always on rivers—we were OK until the final obstacle. It was a particularly wicked mess, with several spindly limbs ready to snatch at feet and ankles. After a tense struggle punctuated with oaths (it was getting dark by then), Pam and I safely crossed and waited on the other side for our companions.

Mar got out first, gingerly assaying the firmness of a soggy ash trunk. "Solid!" she called out, and began pussyfooting along its length, performing the "beaver pond soft shoe." This is a walking technique that attempts to neutralize gravitation. I first heard about it from our neighbor Sooch. He and his buddy Maki used to do a lot of beaver trapping—back in their salad days, when such gory and often frustrating work masqueraded as entertainment. Maki was a big man, not renowned for lightness of foot. He was crossing a frozen beaver pond when he heard the ice split open on the other side. A burgeoning crevice shot his way. He made a dash for shore, prancing on tiptoe. Sooch said Maki lifted his shoulders as if to draw some weight off his feet. He tried to combine feverish haste with a delicate springiness originating at the balls of his feet. In short, he attempted to make himself lighter. It didn't work.

That's how Mar advanced—shoulders hunched up in the antigravity position. She stepped off the first log onto one

·   ·   ·   ·   ·   ·   ·   ·   ·   ·   ·   ·   ·

that also looked sturdy and reliable. It was a careful move, toe first, new eyeglasses glued to the track. Then Mar disappeared. She plunged straight down into the river, forcing two logs apart as she dropped out of sight. It was as if a trapdoor had sprung. There was a modest splash and she was gone.

We gasped, but then her head bobbed back into view almost instantly, and she threw an arm around one of the logs. She sputtered, and hauled herself to the topside of the jam. Neil commented on her good form, but her glasses were gone—forever. Oh sure, Neil made a gallant dive to the bottom, but it was a token effort. The river is stingy with such offerings.

Still, we've scrambled over many logjams since, loath to learn from experience. In that sense we're the close kin of dogs. For example, I've yet to know a rural dog who's suffered a faceful of porcupine quills just once. Wisdom appears to require at least two or three close encounters before the lesson sticks, and some canines never do catch on. The porcupines appear to take it in stride, though sometimes they seem weary.

A few years ago we acquired a puppy. Our old dog had died several months before, and Jim's passing had been so traumatic that we hesitated to initiate yet another cycle of friendship, love, and inevitable loss. How many pets can a human stand to outlive?

But one evening my brother David phoned from Bismarck.

"Do you guys miss Jim?" he asked.

"OK," I replied, "what've you got?"

Well, one night while out partying, David was convinced he should adopt what was billed as a "purebred black lab." In the morning his reasoning capacity returned (temporarily), and he realized that his urban apartment was not prime habitat for what should grow to be a large hunting dog. Out of the goodness of his heart, he decided to give the animal to us.

. . . .

"Tell you what," he cooed, "I'll deliver the dog, his papers, and a month's supply of food, plus I'll take care of the vaccinations."

Reluctantly, Pam and I agreed.

"By the way," David added, "I've already named him 'Bolderev,' after a Czechoslovakian hockey player."

"That's fine," we said. Names are easily changed. ("The Reverend" became one of his nicknames.)

A couple weeks later David arrived with a dog that sported a thatch of ridiculous, wild whiskers sprouting from his chin. It's true the dog was more or less black, but he later proved to be—as near as anyone who was supposed to know could determine—a labrador/airedale cross. Needless to say, the half-breed had no papers on him. Also, David had forgotten the shots, and the dog food spilled on the way. (The pup crawled under the foot pedals of his truck and distracted David to the extent that he swerved off the highway into the ditch.)

Nevertheless, Bolderev won our hearts with pure cuteness and unabashed enthusiasm and affection. Dogs have the Dale Carnegie course programmed into their DNA, and humans are putty in their paws (and tongues). In a few days the dog was fully ours, or vice versa, at home and content. But we knew it was only a matter of time before he met his first porcupine.

It happened six months later, in the dead of winter. A porcupine moved into our garage, attracted by the road salt on the car. The fenders and mud flaps were accessible and tasty—good enough to lick. Bolderev charged in, growling with the hot zeal of his predator ancestors. He darted out yelping, probably more frightened than hurting. The real pain was yet to come.

He had about a dozen-and-a-half quills protruding from his nose, lips, and tongue, but we'd seen much worse. Enough quills can be fatal—preventing eating and drinking—and one of our previous dogs had so many, so deep (some at the back of the throat), that we were forced to hurry him into the vet for a full anesthetic in order to extract them all. And he'd procured them from a *dead* porcupine by the side of the road. For Bolderev it looked like outpatient work. Pam fetched the pliers.

I outweighed the dog by at least five times, and I could blanket his entire body with my torso. From past operations we understood there was nothing to be gained from subtlety. I flopped Bolderev flat on his side on the back porch, and then lay on top of him, bringing most of my weight to bear. I clutched his head in both hands, tensed every muscle, and whispered irrelevant reassurances into his earflap. Pam tenderly patted his brow, then yanked out the first bloody quill.

The dog convulsed in pain and terror. It was like lying atop a single, massive knot of muscle—that's wired into a 220-volt socket. All my strength was required to ride the bucking dog and keep a grip on his head. It was clear he desired to bite me. Winning friends and influencing humans was now far less important than ripping a chunk out of one.

Small wonder. A quill is hard and needle-like, with a wicked little barb at the end. They pierce flesh easily and take root like fish hooks. Pulling quills is not unlike pulling teeth—physically and metaphorically—and if we'd had some nitrous oxide lying around, I would've administered a healthy dose to Bolderev. (And the rest to us.)

As it was, we vicariously shared his pain, and he struggled so violently that we thought it best to pluck half the quills and give it a rest. I let him up and he bolted off the porch and into the woods. But in a minute he was back, wagging his tail and jostling my leg. Dogs can't help it. They're slaves to devotion—abject and blind.

We petted him and told him he was good (a distortion), but when he started pawing at his face again, we decided to go for the balance of the stickers immediately. It's easy for a victim to snap the shafts off the quills, and then it's almost impossible to snag them with pliers.

After several minutes of torture, we finally wore Bolderev out, and Pam managed to extract the rest of the barbs. She had a small pile of trophies on the floor. They were pretty. The pointed end is black, shading to dark brown about a half-inch back. It has ultrafine bristles, which you can only feel if you run a finger toward the point—all the better to grip pierced tissue. The rest of the quill is ivory white and about two inches long. It seems to be made of the same hard, shiny material as the shafts of bird feathers. They look like tiny, streamlined javelins, well designed and businesslike. Pam scooped them up and held her hand under Bolderev's bleeding nose. He wrinkled his snout and backed away. Perhaps this crude surgery had stamped a lasting impression.

And mirabile dictu!, three days later the porcupine was back in the garage, and, though Bolderev found it, he didn't get "quilled." He was content to bark at the porcupine and make short, false charges at its head. Was this a dog who had actually learned the cruel lesson of the quills? We were very pleased.

But he was playing a dangerous game, so Pam called him into the house, and I marched out to evict the porcupine.

We didn't begrudge this fat rodent its treat of Minnesota Highway Department salt, but the delicacy would have to be savored elsewhere. The porcupine was huddled near the left front tire of the car, and didn't appear to be in a hurry to leave. We'd recently put down some wood flooring in the house, so I grabbed a long scrap of one-by-two oak board to use as a prod. I approached Porky from behind (contrary to popular fable, they *cannot* launch their quills like Scuds) and tapped him gently on the back. To my amazement a half-dozen quills were instantly embedded in the board. It's a difficult trick to violate oak with a hammer and nails. I was glad I hadn't used the toe of my boot. Pam would've been quick with the pliers, but who would have held me down on the porch?

Porky waddled a few feet and halted. I suppose he felt some quills leave their sheathes and assumed another pest had been discouraged. Besides, he had a lot more barbs where those came from.

·   ·   ·   ·   ·   ·   ·   ·   ·   ·   ·   ·   ·

The Snow Lotus

I tapped him again. He shuffled another dozen steps. And that was how we played the game for fifty yards down the driveway. Tap, waddle, stop. It was like a cartoon caricature of a bizarre hockey game, with the porcupine as an anemic, but especially hazardous, puck. Pam laughed from the back steps, crying, "Don't hurt him! Don't hurt him!" as Porky grunted and stumbled and finally mounted the snowbank at the edge of our road. He had a rough time scaling the precipitous, two-and-a-half-foot ridge, and I was tempted to boost him with the end of the board. But I figured I'd consumed enough of his quills; he might need a batch to ward off a fox or a wolf.

Right. What he actually needed them for was Bolderev's postgraduate education. Porky returned to the garage next day, and our latest dog joined the ranks of his predecessors in the Two-Time Quill Club. We heard a pathetic whine and rushed to the back door. Bolderev was crouched on the bottom step, displaying a full beard of quills and a sheepish slant to his eyes.

I told him what he was—loudly and explicitly—as Pam fetched the pliers.

A half hour later I stepped over an exhausted, chastened dog curled up on the back porch rug, and strode out to the garage. Wielding the oak board, I herded Porky down the driveway again, this time twice as far. He didn't return. I guess he was tired of graciously teaching our dog the facts of backwoods life, only to be rudely hustled away for his trouble.

Shakespeare wrote: "Nature teaches beasts to know their friends." Absolutely. For canines, they are bipedal, hairless mammals who reek of coffee and deodorant, and sometimes brandish pliers. Our devotion is touching, but it's often nasty business.

A few years ago *The New Republic* magazine ran a cover story entitled "The Idiocy of Rural Life," and responding to the predictable uproar, featured another cover story a month later, "The Idiocy of Urban Life." (I anxiously awaited the logical culmination of the series—"The Idiocy of Life, Period"—but unfortunately it never appeared.)

The first article was prefaced with a bon mot by Marx and Engels from *The Communist Manifesto*: "The bourgeoisie has subjected the country to the rule of the town. It has created enormous cities, has greatly increased the urban population as compared with the rural, and has thus rescued a considerable part of the population from the idiocy of rural life."

I like that. I hope all urban folk take it to heart and relinquish any fantasies they may entertain about "getting back to the land" (or *lakeshore,* more likely). It's mean out here—cruel and bloody, as I've demonstrated above. Besides, prices are high and incomes are low. Forget the romance.

For instance, as a town-bred child myself, I thought it would be the pinnacle of backwoods life to be a game warden—constantly cruising the forests and waterways, protecting our furry and feathered friends—a cross beween Davy Crockett and Mr. Rogers. I vaguely recall a series of young-adult novels featuring a game warden as the heroic protagonist. I could see it.

But as the years passed I discovered that a significant portion of the human species despises and fears game wardens, and that our animal friends are, at best, indifferent. If my youthful fantasy bubble needed further puncture, it happened last spring. I was working the fire season at the local Department of Natural Resources forestry station when a game warden (they're called "conservation officers" these days) drove up towing his government boat trailer. It was the day before the Fishing Opener, and he was preparing for the seasonal rush of weekend warriors. The Fishing Opener is akin to, in an urban setting, gridlock downtown, or a huge street demonstration on the verge of open riot.

The warden was adding air to the spare tire for his trailer when he looked up at me and grimaced.

"I don't know why I'm bothering to fill this spare," he said, "I don't have a jack."

.   .   .   .

I cheerfully suggested that it was still best to have the extra tire ready, since he could always flag down a citizen and borrow a jack if necessary.

He stared at me, eyes brimming with pity at my naïveté.

"Someone stop and help *me?*" He chuckled bitterly. "Saddam Hussein would have a better chance."

I laughed. It was true. Protecting walleyes (and Bambi and Thumper and Yogi) is nasty business.

So if you live in the city and sometimes feel the urge to chuck it all and dwell in the woods, give me a call. I'll let you use the pliers before we paddle down the Sturgeon, and then maybe we'll fire up the sauna. It'll be great. Make sure you have a jack (and a job), and a high tolerance for idiocy.

Of course, if you want to stay in the city that'll be fine.

Oh, by the way, did I mention the ticks that carry Lyme disease? The mosquitoes that transmit encephalitis? The rabid skunks? I know, I know, leave it to a writer to glorify things.

⑤ Total Eclipse
of the Clouds

Fever itself is Nature's instrument.
Thomas Sydenham

The illness punched me. I was stretched out in front of the woodstove, watching a video, and as I stood up, chills consumed me instantly. I shuddered, teeth chattering, and Pam stared from across the room. We were astounded by the sudden violence. My only warning had been a vague scratchiness at the back of the throat, but until the moment of assault I felt fine—had skied five miles cross-country only hours before.

The first wave of shivers passed, and I started upstairs. But on the second step a downdraft swept by, and the chills returned in a fury. I hugged myself, heeding the ominous telegraph of clacking teeth. Through the spasms I muttered, "This is amazing. I've never been mugged by a virus before."

I staggered up to the bedroom, now intensely feverish as well. Pam followed, palming my forehead as I burrowed under a quilt.

"Feels like a strong fever brewing," she said. "I'll take your temperature in a little while."

The sickness engendered the usual sense of betrayal, and a general aura of insecurity—a vivid mnemonic of how vulnerable, how *biological* we are, subject to personal extinction. For a moment I rallied, putting on a macho face: "Well, maybe I'll have some interesting hallucinations at least." Pam offered the grimace she usually reserves for inane jock interviews on TV.

Then I gradually descended into that twilight zone of fever and chills where the arrow of time abandons purpose and sequence, and space shrinks to a cocoon of mattress, pillow, and covers. And I did hallucinate—or so lucidly dream that what the images actually were boils down to semantics. At some point I was distantly aware that Pam came to bed, but the rest of the night, which seemed in retrospect to have endured for days, was a magical mystery tour of waking sleep. I seemed to slip in and out of consciousness, ever returning to the same theme: THREE. Manifestations of the numeral coiled around and twisted through a surreal Native American backdrop of dancers, council fires, and a chanting shaman. Many times I was certain my eyes were open, but I still viewed the dream—warmly illuminated by lunar radiation suffusing our bedroom. I hazily recalled that the moon was near full.

After midnight, I think, Pam went to the bathroom and, when she returned, stood before the bedroom window and murmured, "There's a pair of flying squirrels on the bird feeder." They were briefly incorporated into my images.

A few minutes later (or several, who could tell?) I made the same trip, and as I gazed out the window the reality of the winter night temporarily jostled the dreaming aside.

.   .   .   .

The forest was snow-covered, and ethereally dazzling beneath the late-November moon. The fir trees were crystalline spires, and even stark shadows were brightened by reflected light. I looked down, hoping to spot the flying squirrels, but instead I saw two deer, ghostly in the lunar effulgence, fully exposed in the yard, with noses pushed into the snow beneath the feeder. I gasped at their beauty and hoarsely whispered, "Pam, deer!" like I'd never seen one before. They heard me through the membrane of glass and bolted into the woods—shades and silhouettes vanishing beneath the laden boughs of a balsam fir. I've witnessed countless deer at night, but all in the glare of headlights; I had never glimpsed them in moon glow, in their natural demeanor of phantoms.

Pam started to rise.

"Never mind," I said. "They're gone."

Shivering, I returned to the hot nest of the quilt and focused once more on the fever. Soon I arrived back at THREE, reeling through protean visions that seemed terribly important, but that I didn't understand, and recalled only nebulously when dawn finally painted the window pink.

It was ten degrees below zero, and since we heat with two woodstoves, Pam and I struggled to light one apiece. She'd had a 103-degree fever of her own two days before, and was not completely recovered. It was grim labor. What if, I wondered, we were both too sick to split kindling and haul wood? What if one of us were alone and very old? I shoved the thought aside.

I spent most of the day in bed, drifting at the edge of awareness. Each time my eyes opened I realized a soupy blackness had settled over my mind, seeping out into the room like a pall of smog, dimming the windowpane. The radio was on, but every tune was a threnody, mocking my frailty, heralding the slow, inevitable decay.

I thought of Jim, a college classmate we hadn't seen for several years. Word had arrived the month before that he was dead at age forty-three, killed by ALS, Lou Gehrig's dis-

. . . .

ease, after a debilitating decline. He'd sought alternative therapies as far away as Europe, not accepting the death sentence pronounced by his doctor. It was to no avail. Pam said later that she too meditated on his fate during her illness—and on the unfolding realization that she was now past forty, and that as usual in November, we'd enjoyed precious little sunshine. Just after sunrise, clouds had rolled in again. In this region it's statistically the most overcast month, and whenever I think of Thanksgiving, I see the long string of seasons and dinners in muted shades of gray. That, I realized, is how I shall also see Jim.

In early evening the clouds were briefly torn, allowing a ragged glimpse of pale dusk from the bedroom window. My mood lifted to see the slash of yellow along the western horizon. A total lunar eclipse would commence just after 10:30 P.M., and peak around midnight. We'd been anticipating the event for weeks, and I was worried that the ubiquitous clouds would mask it. I bitterly recall the fabulous Leonid meteor shower (November 17th) of 1966—one of the most memorable celestial events of the century (up to one hundred meteors per second at one point)—that I missed because of November murk. This eclipse, I decided, would be the highlight of the season, and perhaps now a healing event as well—something to break the fever, at least symbolically, and distract my vision from treacherous biology.

But by 7:00 P.M. the clouds regrouped, and the overcast appeared to be thick and seamless. So much for the eclipse, my longed-for heavenly menhir, and omen of better days.

My second night of sickness wore on, not quite as feverish or vivid; THREE did not reappear. But despite the overcast, our bedroom was bright. The full moon beyond the clouds was still setting the landscape aglow. The sky, the snow, our sheets, were all the same amorphous tint of dull silver.

Just after midnight I awoke from a fitful shift of incoherent dreams. Pam was awake and felt me stir.

"Look," she said, "it's dark now."

. . . .

The room was black, the window nearly opaque. A patch of sky visible through the glass was the muddiest gray, only discernible in contrast to the deep shadow of the room.

"It's the eclipse," I said. "It's reached totality."

I groaned my way out of bed and stumbled to the window. Still overcast. But what loveliness must reign above the cloud deck; how stupendous it would be to soar through the overcast and burst into a starscape dominated by the red-orange aura of the eclipse. I could imagine it: navigating a crisp nocturnal sky, the continent of clouds below stained rose by enameled moonlight. How wonderful it would feel to be flying this night. How wonderful it would feel to be well. But the eclipse did not cool my fever.

"Most of the time we think we're sick," wrote Thomas Wolfe, "it's all in the mind." Perhaps. But I also believe that most of the time we think we're healthy, it's also in the mind.

In any case, I'm fine now (at least for a while), the virus mugger overpowered; and I've resolved to pay closer attention to THREE.

.   .   .   .

⑤ Blood Walk

.
.
.
.
.
.
.
.
.
.
.

You are like dogs in the Hot Moon when they run mad and snap at their own shadows.
LITTLE CROW

I walked twenty-five miles in a wet snowfall. The route was a labyrinthine trek through the streets of Mankato, Minnesota, a town I'd never seen before I stepped off the bus that morning. I was issued a crude map, but it was nearly useless, and soon smeared. I was at the mercy of small, handmade signs and arrows—stuck in snowbanks, or tacked to boulevard elms and maples. They were difficult to discern through the screen of swirling snowflakes, and after about fifteen miles I began to feel the full consequences of my fast. I was weak, my senses bleary, forced to concentrate intently on each twist and turn, peering anxiously ahead to spot the signs. They read—laconically, aptly—"Walk."

This long march was sponsored by The American Freedom from Hunger Foundation, and billed as a "Walk for Development." Our official motto for the day: "Walk hunger off the world." Each participant had garnered sponsors who pledged so much money per mile tallied, with the proceeds to be delivered to the needy in Guatemala. It was early December 1969, and I was an idealistic college freshman worried about the world. Between my personal pledge and that of an old employer, I was worth twenty-five cents per mile. Even a quarter-century ago, it was a widow's mite, but there were hundreds of us out on the streets that day.

I noted the irony shadowing my presence in Mankato. One of the organizations responsible for the project was the Catholic Church, a denomination that had molded my youth, and that I had decisively left only four months before. I was now affiliated with a fundamentalist Protestant sect that had convinced me, among other things, that the true Christian sabbath should be strictly observed from sundown Friday to sundown Saturday, and the period was dedicated exclusively to worship. No work, no play. I had passed the several preceding Saturdays studying the Bible, praying, meditating, and, not least, fasting. I lost twenty pounds, and when my mother saw me at Christmas break two weeks later, she was horrified. At six-foot-three, and down to 165, I looked like death. My cheeks were hollow, my frame gaunt, none of my clothing fit. And I didn't put on weight in Mankato. By then I was gradually slipping into a compulsive asceticism.

Because The Walk was on a Saturday, I had a problem. Due to the exertion, and the time involved, I wasn't sure if it was an acceptable sabbath activity. I agonized for days, not wishing to offend God or my conscience, and finally (and uncomfortably) decided that since it was for a worthy,

.   .   .   .

Christian-like cause, it was OK—with one caveat: I must pray the entire time, and think only of God.

The long bus ride from the College of St. Thomas in St. Paul was an ordeal. My fellow students were buoyant and talkative, on a lark. It was secular chatter, and therefore I was forbidden to take part on the sabbath. I hunched into a window seat and pressed my face to the glass, apparently absorbed in the scenery—blustery darkness—only speaking if directly addressed, and then in monosyllables. I was soon left alone. The other trial was food. I had begun my latest fast the previous evening, and everyone else had packed a lunch for the ride. The guy next to me had stopped at Burger King, and the rich aroma from his takeout bag mocked my pangs and laid a keen edge on my natural, but despised, desire. He offered me some fries, but I said I wasn't hungry. (Yeah, right.) I was tempted to opine about our mission to combat hunger, and draw some vague analogy about empathy and shared privation, but that would have been prideful, and hence a sin.

So for me, the twenty-five-mile walk on an empty stomach was a special physical challenge, but nevertheless a sideshow. I was also engaged in a gritty contest of wills. While my legs—increasingly remote and unreal—pushed steadily on through the maze of snowy sidewalks and intersections, my mind roiled, at war with itself.

One combatant was the will to keep my personal vow and think only religious thoughts for the entire walk. The other was the tendency of the mind to wander, prodded by hunger, weariness, and simple normal function, into channels that did not honor the sabbath—an unrequited romantic infatuation, my seatmate's hamburger, science fiction fantasies from years before, curiosity about people and buildings passed on the street, my seatmate's hamburger. . . . Stop! I would catch myself. No! Stay focused on God. I recited Bible verses, imagined prophetic events, confessed my failings, professed admiration for creation—all to keep clean, to sanctify the day. It was a seesaw battle, and I

.   .   .   .

churned through the hours, swinging from the ethereal and divine to the base cravings of the body.

I walked alone, partly because I quickly outdistanced our busload, and partly because a satisfied, deliberate loneliness was manifest in my bearing. God was my companion, and he took up a lot of space. Twenty-five miles, and I never spoke, retracted almost completely into the battleground of the spirit.

Five days before, I had visited my cousin Michael in a Twin Cities hospital. He'd been in a car accident, and his jaw was wired together. He couldn't speak. He seemed to be in rough shape, and how different was the character of his silence. Also imposed by God? We were both eighteen. I prayed for him.

A few weeks earlier, I received my new draft card in the mail—a II-S deferment. No telling how long that would be golden, but it didn't really matter. I was a pacifist now. Only God had the right to wage war, and I prayed about Vietnam. I knew I wouldn't go. My Bible study counseled me to choose prison if need be. I was temporarily aglow with a vicarious appreciation of martyrdom.

And what a contrast between this region and the planet Arrakis—so much moisture here. The Fremen wouldn't thrive in the Midwest without their mandatory desert hardship, though the Pentagon could probably provide missions aplenty for the Sardauker. And being from northeastern Minnesota, I had always been intrigued by the Harkonnens— expected to see the name on a rural mailbox; did Frank Herbert intend that as a Finnish surname? I remembered our high school physics teacher picking up my copy of *Dune* while we were taking a test. He started to read and was fascinated. I hope he got his own copy and finished it, but it didn't seem likely. . . .

Stop it! Only six or seven miles left. Recite, recite . . . *No one can come to me unless the Father who sent me draws him, and I will raise him up at the last day. . . . Truly, truly, I say to you, unless you eat the flesh of the Son of man and*

.   .   .   .

The Snow Lotus

drink his blood, you have no life in you. . . . It is the spirit that gives life, the flesh is of no avail; the words that I have spoken to you are spirit and life.

Eat the flesh, drink the blood; eat the flesh, drink the blood . . . and I wonder where Debra is right now (playing her violin?), or Kathy and her lovely hair . . . and there before me is my seatmate's hamburger . . . No! Eat the flesh, drink the blood.

Then, somewhere near the end of the walk, after eight hours in the snow and silence, my legs rubbery, my psyche as cratered and contorted as the surface of the moon, I noticed a monument ahead. The snowfall was still heavy, the day was growing dim. The dark pillar loomed out of the gloaming like a rock in a misty river, and I veered off the walk for a better look.

Someone had splashed red paint across its face, and through the stain of "blood" I read the engraving: 38 INDIANS HANGED HERE. I froze and gaped. It was like a fist to the stomach, or a hard slap on the cheek. In my otherworldly, self-possessed state, frail with hunger and weariness, and wracked with guilt over several lapses in prayerful meditation on the sabbath, I could, at first, make little sense of the inscription. Slowly it dawned on me that the thirty-eight were those Sioux executed in the aftermath of what our sixth-grade Minnesota history textbook called the Sioux Uprising of 1862. I recalled that about three hundred Indians had been sentenced to death, but upon review of the cases, President Abraham Lincoln had allowed only thirty-eight to be hanged. It was the largest mass execution in U.S. history.

I stared at the bizarre monument as snow collected on my shoulders and head. I was astonished and appalled that such a thing existed. The red paint did indeed look like blood, and I was glad that someone had vandalized this abomination. . . . That was a Biblical word—"the abomination that maketh desolate" in the Book of Daniel; some said it referred to the unclean blood of a pig sacrificed in the

. . . .

Temple of Jerusalem by Antiochus Epiphanes, and thereafter carried prophetic significance as well. . . . I wondered, had it been an Indian who threw the paint on this ghastly monument? Why didn't they knock it down? . . . Eat the flesh, drink the paint. No, no . . . the blood, the blood.

I had been fighting the thought of food all day—the memory of that cursed hamburger, actually—and now I was certain I couldn't eat. At the end of each sabbath I allowed myself food, and sundown was imminent—or even over, who could tell in that fog of snow? But as I turned away from the pillar—38! INDIANS! HANGED! HERE!— on the last miserable leg of the twenty-five miles (to raise a total of $6.25 for hungry Indians in Guatemala), I had a fix on God, not dinner: eat the flesh, drink the blood; eat the flesh, drink the blood. . . .

As it turned out, I would stay five more years with that fundamentalist sect, even train to be one of their clergy; so I cannot say that my odd encounter with the monument in Mankato turned me on a different path. After all, whatever happened—good or evil—was in some way the will of God, even thirty-eight hanged men. And the next day, back on campus, I watched the Minnesota Vikings beat the Los Angeles Rams on television, then joined a snowball fight with my dormmates; life goes on.

But the experience of that pillar in the December snow was etched into memory, demonstrating not only the tragic injustice of war and racism, but also the selfishness of my personal religious fanaticism. The shock of meeting the monument lingered, reminding me how trivial and childish my inner battle had been that day. It seems to me now that if I had truly wished to honor a sabbath, I might have accepted the french fries, allowing my seatmate the satisfaction of sharing. I might have employed my natural curiosity about people on the street by talking to them, or at least offering a friendly greeting. And I should not have walked for twenty-five miles alone.

.　.　.　.　.　.　.　.　.　.　.　.　.

The Snow Lotus

Carried to extremes, a self-centered religious conviction and regimen can sire bizarre behavior. Recently I heard a radio news report about a person whose devotion and fear attained a dubious rank.

An ambulance crew was called to a residence where they found a man with a bloody face, and one eye missing. The victim explained that while looking into a mirror he saw a pentacle in one eye. (A pentacle is a stylized star symbol that some associate with Satan.) Horrified, the man tried to excise the pentacle with a knife. He gouged out the eyeball and flushed it down the toilet.

Eat the flesh, drink the blood.

⑨ The
Magic Puck

Don't love your life too much.
MARY OLIVER

A few years ago I was offered a full-time job—with benefits. The hourly wage was decent and the work didn't sound onerous. It was income and security we certainly needed. Such offers—out of the blue—are rare.

I turned it down immediately.

Actually, I was surprised at the swiftness of my response. That must mean, I reasoned, that it was the correct decision. But there was irony in the timing. It was the winter solstice, and overcast besides, the darkest day of the year. An omen?

Media pundits were trumpeting recession, and the economic outlook, especially locally, did appear cold and barren. Soon our traditionally frigid New Year's Day would usher in the annum during which I would turn forty—older and less employable, less insurable.

For a moment I was jittery. Had I spoken too quickly? Should I phone back and say I'd changed my mind? I reviewed the original conversation. As the caller described the job, I felt a bolt of panic. The work wasn't menial or superfluous, but it would be monotonous—routine, prescribed, and ultimately boring. I had endured a job like that for a decade, and the stab of fear derived from the realization that I could live it again via a simple "yes." One syllable.

In a rush of images I recalled those bitter, interminable afternoons at the plant, the alarm-ruptured mornings before dawn, the dreary graveyard shifts, and how my metabolism rebelled. And looming over all the tedious labor was the mind-numbing, spirit-crushing predictability. I could project my rigid work calendar far into the future; could know with certainty what shift I'd be manning on January 1, 2001, or March 3, 2029—and where I would be and what I'd be doing. My life was scheduled. I could plot my swing shifts like a sine wave on graph paper, as regular as the rotation of the earth, the pattern to be broken only by retirement or death. It was an enervating, paralyzing concept. I turned down the job offer because I wished to avoid that niche, that cage, at almost any cost, and choose freedom. But it would have been so easy to say "yes."

That's why I keep a hockey puck on the dashboard of my car. I unceremoniously tossed it there after my final hockey game. I'm retired from the "adult league"—couldn't take the punishment anymore—but I left the puck there as a reminder of fleeting youth. It's my *momento mori*. If a passenger picks it up and asks, "What's this doing here?" I say: "That's the magic puck, it reveals the future. Go ahead, gaze into it. What do you see? It's all black, right? Well, that's the future: death." I shrug and grin fatalistically, forgiving the

· · · · · · · · · · · · · ·

The Snow Lotus

triteness of the moment. I explain how medieval monks kept human skulls in their cells for the same purpose. "The magic puck reminds me that no matter what I do in life, the ultimate result is the same: death. That being the case, I may as well 'go for the gusto,' take risks, and live it to the hilt—flat-out-to-the-max."

So my refusal was reflexive. I rationalized the jitters, chiding myself to think of the future—the dense vision of the magic puck. "Gusto" does not include being shackled to a mandated, life-corralling routine. There's nothing more toxic to zest and joy than the treadmill of a "formal" job that isn't challenging. Beyond the drab, relentless organization of your life is the fact that you are owned. *Employee* derives from the Old French *emplier*, which means "to fold in," as with weaving. Thus, an employee is "woven" into an organization, tangled (often inextricably) into a complex web of obligation and dependence. The difference between an employee and an indentured servant (or a slave) is only a matter of degree.

I vividly remember how Jimmy looked when I relieved him at dawn after yet another shift at the plant. He'd put in fifteen years, and had at least fifteen to go. He appeared worn and listless, overcome by apathy, and trapped for life by economic pressures. It was a haunted, depressing aspect, and it scared the hell out of me. Is that how I looked?

My last shift at the plant was one of the truly joyous days of my life—my "re-birthday"—and I threw a party for those who remained. I arrived at work laden with goodies, and we celebrated my new life with soft drinks and everyone's favorite deli sandwiches. It was a big day for the others, too. Once clasped in the arms of the plant (decent wages, great benefits, rock-solid job security), no one ever quit. My voluntary departure was a singular event, a bold insult to routine that made people giddy.

Both serendipitous and intended circumstances made this sea change possible. Pam had landed a good job with a Fortune 500 company, we had no mortgage, we were

· · · · · · · · · · · · · · ·

childfree, and I had a marketable writing skill coupled with a hot desire to use it. (Desire is as critical as skill.) So I had a parachute, and I bailed out.

Unfortunately, the canopy quickly collapsed. Pam's employer fell on lean times—or at least perceived lean times—and her position was eliminated. Suddenly, we were faced with an old-fashioned, rugged-individualism brand of independence. Hard times commenced; gritty, mean, sometimes bitter. Our mutual freelance income dipped below the official poverty line, and for the first time in our working lives we weren't liable for income tax. That's one of the surest signs your lifestyle has swerved out of the American mainstream. Our garden became a significant source of groceries, and due to the inherent irregularity of paydays, remittances to our creditors slipped into arrears. The bank initiated repossession of our car, the power company threatened shutoff, and AT&T, one of the most potent corporations on the globe, turned us over to a collection agency for a forty-six-dollar long-distance bill that we'd promised to pay at the earliest opportunity. Bastards.

When you're poor you are automatically thrust into an adversarial relationship with the business community. They have what you need, but you don't have what they need—it's why poverty is referred to as a struggle. No one wants to see you suffer (except maybe AT&T), but they can't be thrilled about extending credit either.

Once I was owed over two thousand dollars by the U.S. government, but payment would take six weeks, and we were flat-ass broke, so I approached a banker with documentation of the government's obligation. I asked for a one-thousand-dollar loan to tide us over until the check arrived. We had taken out four loans from that bank in more prosperous days, and repaid them all on schedule—in one case, ahead of schedule. However, as the banker was quick to note, we'd been *late* with *two* payments on a loan at another institution, and on the strength of that blasphemous performance, he denied the loan. On black days I indulged

. . . .

in a dark fantasy about that bank. It involved automatic weapons, explosives, and hostages. An old song by The Hollies cycled through my head: "I'll Pay You Back with Interest."

On the other hand, we were blessed. It was extremely difficult, if not impossible, to sink into debt. Without the aid of bankers one is forced to be financially responsible, and if something is unaffordable you simply survive without — freedom from desire. It's appealingly Zen-like. There's little incentive to pine for the unattainable.

That's the message of The Magic Puck: by knowing the end, you are free to design the middle. And the more that's a struggle, the freer you become. It's a paradox. The greater limits you face, the greater your opportunity for freedom. It's like this: we have all been assured at one time or another, "You can accomplish anything you want if you try hard enough." Bullsnot. The thing I desire to do more than all else is to climb to the rim of a high cliff and dive off, soaring away like an osprey, flying and gliding like an eagle. If I actually make that leap, I'm dead, regardless of desire or effort. However, that same lust for seemingly impossible flight has spurred other humans to create aircraft, spacecraft, perhaps someday a starship.

There *are* limits. The ultimate barrier is death. No matter what I do or who I am, I shall eventually arrive in its shadow. So why approach on tiptoe? Why spend a life attempting to preserve a life which can by no means be preserved? The scramble for affluence and security arises out of a yen for self-preservation, a goal that is, in the end, futile. Jung wrote: "The goal is important only as an idea; the essential thing is the *opus* which leads to the goal; that is the goal of a lifetime."

In other words, focus on the process, concentrate on the *living*. Go for it. Refuse, in my case, a boring, tedious job. True, it guarantees more difficulties, but, "Man," [Jung again] "needs difficulties; they are necessary for health." Just be sure to choose the right difficulties. Surviving a

.   .   .   .

decade of swing shifts was difficult, but it wasn't healthy. Only *stopping* the swings was wholesome.

During a writing class I was giving to hopeful, earnest students I was asked: "You're telling me how to start, and that's great, but how do I know when to quit?" Excellent question. The short answer is *never*. But that's too flippant—how much punishment is enough? We do have to feed our families and pay our phone bills. I waffled over a reply, talked about setting personal timetables and professional goals, and came up with nothing satisfactory. That was before I had fully contemplated the future. Now I would tell the student about The Magic Puck and how it spurs me to continue on the torturous path of freedom. It will one day lead to dissolution, but *all* paths go there. The time to quit, therefore, is when you no longer relish the path.

And maybe one day I will quit, but every time I get in the car The Magic Puck reminds me that the destination is the same—obvious, old, and well-known. So I try to relax and enjoy the ride.

But having said all that, having preached defiance of the shadow of death and the humdrum status quo, I must admit to a dark longing. Sometimes, when freedom seems too brutal and costly, I feel a throb of nostalgia for the night shift. It passes quickly, and I'll never go back, but occasionally I have the urge to flip the damn puck out the window (at highway speed), hurry to the employment office, and latch onto somebody's permanent payroll. To hell with the future! Let's nail down some security.

My salvation is that it's too late. I've been out of the mainstream for so long that my life has become subversive. I couldn't be permanently woven into an organization. I couldn't be a regular employee, but only a saboteur, a malcontent, a generator of negative waves. I have been to The Promised Land. I'm spoiled rotten for conventional jobs, and useless to the socioeconomic zeitgeist. Someone has to build the cars, can the food, treat the sewage, but it's no longer me. I am, in the eyes of many, a derelict. So be it.

. . . .

The Snow Lotus

It doesn't require courage to gaze into The Magic Puck, only memory. As long as I remember what the night shift at the sewage plant was really like, I'll be able to live with the uncertainty of the present and the certainty of the future. Gusto is good—to the very last drop.

I hope.

⑨ Tilting Round the Far Spruce

The moon and I could keep this up forever.
F. P. A.

Like an alchemist with his stone, I carried my skis to the edge of the bog that rings Secret Lake. It was January 28th, and if not for the trail I'd been tramping since early November, I would have wallowed past my knees in snow.

"I went out to the hazel wood," wrote W. B. Yeats, "Because a fire was in my head." *I* went out onto the frozen lake because there was a glow in the east—moonrise. And because there was a fire in my head. If Yeats meant a longing for wonder and a restlessness of mind that drives poetry and

127

prayer, then I understand his longing, and the mission of his "wandering Aengus."

I know there are sparks in the snow crystals. A northwest wind, fresh blue from the Arctic and colder than icebergs, can sting like a match to the lips. I am drawn to such heat. Though it was two hours after sundown, the air temperature hovered at seven degrees above, almost luxuriously mild in the wake of an eight-day span when the daily highs never reached zero, and bottomed out at minus forty. It was a grim, exhilarating winter. Lake Superior, 31,000 square miles in area and 1,300 feet deep, froze over completely for the first time in fifteen seasons.

The character of daily life is enhanced by such cold. Thoughtless routine shades into a regimen of survival. If I failed to haul firewood into the house, we would die. If my truck swerved into the ditch on some remote, icy road, and I wasn't properly dressed or equipped, I might lose fingers or toes, or perhaps die. Carelessness or bad luck that would cause mere inconvenience or irritation in Hawaii or southern California can kill you in northern Minnesota. This awareness hones the senses.

One of my ski tracks headed straight off across the lake, and that's the one I followed, poling to the west through an inch of fresh snow, my back to the moon. To maximize the effect of its rising, I wouldn't face the lunar disk until I was a quarter mile or so out onto the snowfield of the lake—beyond the opaque influence of the forest, and rimmed by full-fledged horizon.

After three or four minutes I paused. Ahead was the Great Square of Pegasus and the curving horn of Andromeda, tilting round the celestial pole toward the tops of the far spruce. In the great circle of the year these constellations represent October, vestiges of autumn long gone and barely remembered. Overhead was deep winter—Taurus and the Pleiades—and rising with the moon, I knew, was Regulus and the head of Leo, a distant mirage of April.

I kicked my right ski straight up and twisted it around,

.   .   .   .

following with the left, watching the tips. I planted the poles and slowly raised my face.

The moon was a hot uranic blossom. Its brilliance erased all but the brightest stars from the eastern sky, transfusing the blush of lunar glow toward the upraised arm of Orion. The moon was an outstretched handbreadth above the forest, and long, radiating shadows of aspen and fir speared out onto the lake in a bristling semicircle of darkness. The snowfield, so flat and smooth beneath the noonday sun, revealed its true nature in the magnification of low-angle moonbeams. It was rippled, mottled black and white and glinting. The merest irregularity, the wispiest ridge of wind-cast flakes, was highlighted and projected outward from the arc lamp of the lunar disk. The phase was thirty-six hours past full, with a dark smudge on the upper limb of the orb, the first hint of the waning toward New Moon and the birth of the next cycle.

I drew in a long breath, relishing the raw freshness of polar air, and exhaled with a sigh born of the inability to truly grasp the joy of beauty. I recalled an anecdote related many years before by an old friend. He told of snowshoeing near Lake Tahoe on a clear morning after a blizzard, the conifers laden with snow, the open lake an azure sky come to earth. He was so overwhelmed he wept, helpless to absorb the spectacle.

I was in that state. Though the tears didn't reach my cheeks (where the wind would freeze them), I felt their pressure, and decided the source was frustration. I was experiencing the beauty, but I was too aware of identity — experiencing myself experiencing the artistry, like trying to read sentences while focusing on each letter. I clung to the margin of that spectacular moonrise, locked into a narrow perspective: a male human out on the ice, 1,370 feet above sea level, with eyes, skin, and ears constructed in a certain unalterable manner, and capable of a lifespan that is astronomically and geologically insignificant. True, my sapiens brain/mind is a biological marvel, but it seems just powerful

.   .   .   .

enough to vividly reveal what I do not know and cannot do. It was glorious to watch the moonrise, but insufficient. I wanted to *make* the moon rise, I wanted to *be* the moonrise.

It's an ancient yen. In what we presume to label "primitive" religion, connoting not only "earliness," but also "crudeness" and "inferiority," the notion of *shapeshifting* was common. A shaman or priest could gain wisdom and power by changing into an animal, the wind, or some other manifestation of the natural world. Was it based on a longing for a divergent perspective? Was it engendered by the pain of untouchable beauty?

The self is in the way—mediating, filtering, and categorizing experience. Shifting shape would temporarily banish the self, allowing approach from the margins to the core, or at least the vision of an entirely different margin. That would be divine.

But despite desire and the ache of joy, I remained fixed in my ski bindings, fully human. It was, of course, a privilege to be blessed by the suffering of beauty, pining for keener insight and reveling in the rigors of a peaceful winter. Because, a week before, news reports out of Sarajevo had again shocked the world. A covey of children, frolicking in the snow, had been ripped apart by an artillery shell. Six were killed, others maimed. How different were our snowscapes. I saw a fleeting television image of a man with a shovel working over a great splotch of blood in a snowbank. It wasn't clear if he intended to pile fresh white on top, or to dig the crimson stain out of the bank. I recalled the winter play of childhood, and how my pals and I so loved the snow—sliding, tunneling, rolling, building—carefree and secure. I tried to imagine a 120mm mortar round whistling into our midst on the sledding hill below the water tower in Chisholm; John decapitated, Bob shredded, Dicky shrieking. Impossible.

I pushed off my poles and skied toward the moon. Across the pure expanse of the ice sheet, thousands of crystals twinkled in the waxing moonshine. I shook my head like an irritated dog, an involuntary and futile attempt to clear my head of horrible images.

Shapeshifting? Yes, how awesome to *be* the wind. But much better, I think, to change briefly into a crippled child, or into a bent man with a bloody shovel. If we all could really master that — the projection of our personalities into the worldviews and nervous systems of other humans — then artillery itself might eventually become rare and exotic. We already have a word for the phenomenon — *empathy* — so there's hope. Naming something is the first stage in understanding it.

Yet, as I stepped out of my skis at the edge of the forest, I realized that while I can name "joy," I'm not certain what it is. Beauty brought tears to my eyes! I love the sky, the trees, the snow, and even the cold. Do they love me? I don't think so. The love is unrequited. When I am gone I won't be missed by the world. That's why I watch the moon rise now. That's why the present moment is a snapshot of divinity.

Next morning The Reverend and I walked down to the lake as the sun rose. We both paused at the edge of the forest to urinate. It was minus twenty-six degrees, and as I bored a yellowish hole in the snow pack, I noticed the wave of sunlit steam generated by the arc of piss. It was like an undulating flag of mist, wafting away to rejoin the atmosphere. It was beautiful. I laughed. Joy may be tenuous, but I readily grasp the humor of everyday perception.

The dog paid no heed to his yellow stain. As soon as he was done he ran back up to the house, briefly lifting one paw, then the other. His feet were cold. Right now.

.   .   .   .

⑤ An
Easy Winter

.
.
.
.
.
.
.
.
.
.
.

To which I make my way eating the silence of animals
Offering snow to the darkness
Today belongs to few and tomorrow to no one.
W. S. MERWIN

It was a mild winter with little snow—an easy one—but I
felt lucky to see the spring. Some didn't make it.

We drove into that winter on December 1st, winding
down the Stingy Lake Forest Road with the headlights off.
A misting of snow had painted the gravel white and left the
forest black. The snowfall vanished into the woods, settling
delicately on leaf litter and needle duff, invisible from the
car, and the road was like a milky stream twisting through

133

the trees. The halogen beams glared off the crystals, so I killed the lights and slowed down. As our eyes adjusted to darkness, the white road/river was simple to navigate, and on a Thursday night other human traffic on the Stingy route was improbable.

A few miles south of our cabin, where the Blandin Paper Company manufactured a huge clearcut, the northern horizon briefly opened and we glimpsed an arc of the aurora borealis. We were headed that way on a river of snow.

The ride was a seasonal baptism, with each mile along the Stingy seeming to immerse us deeper into the challenge of winter, acclimating us to the long nights, the lovely and treacherous snow, the necessary evil of hibernal driving. This, I told Pam, was a fair measure of our quality of life: how far can we safely drive without headlights? The question addresses population density and the color of the dirt road, and both parameters are linked to winter. To live in a territory lacking the hard focus of a serious cold season seems to me an almost crippling disadvantage. A northern winter is a clean, worthy adversary, and an honest friend. It's the whetstone of a keen-edged life, and a paladin of solitude. Constant warmth and dependable sunshine generate suburbs and freeways as surely as feces in a petri dish produce colonies of *E. coli*. Even our hard winters are a charm compared to urban sprawl and congestion, where enemies only subvert and solitude has no champion.

But this winter flaunted the charms of a trickster, the crooked grin of Coyote. It was mellow, yes—but only in the weather reports. We clucked our amazement at the afternoon highs, but such was not the true heart of that season.

All December I gambled, and blessed the end of the wretched Christmas shopping spree. I was on a book-signing tour, crisscrossing Minnesota in my light, two-wheel-drive pickup, vainly hoping that the concrete blocks I'd laid in the box would provide an extra edge of traction and security when the highways and shopping mall parking lots turned ugly.

I don't know many writers who relish the histrionics of a book tour, the mandatory dispensing of smiles and autographs when you'd much rather be writing a new book, or perhaps be *thinking* about writing while watching the woodstove glow. But publishers love the hell out of book tours, and it pays—at least theoretically—to keep their publicists happy.

So on December 15th I steered for Bemidji—about 110 miles away—peering through blowing sleet on notorious U.S. Highway 2, a deadly artery of commerce where the tractor-trailers are as thick as flies on roadkill. The semis were unaffected by the smear of slush on the asphalt, but my little Toyota, buffeted by northwest wind, was yearning to cross the centerline or careen into the ditch. After the first fishtail of my rear wheels I slowed to 45 mph. The big trucks blew by in both directions, splattering my windshield with salty crud. I hoped I had a full reservoir of washer fluid, and that all the truck drivers had had enough caffeine.

I arrived at the designated bookstore with my vehicle intact, but my mood befouled—not that it was terribly effervescent in the first place. Even though it was only a silent complaint in my head, I ordered myself to stop whining: there are probably thousands of would-be authors out in the wide moonscape of American literary lust who would kill to have a book-signing gig. Still, it seemed silly that in two hours I would be back out on Highway 2, with whitened knuckles glued to the steering wheel.

I recalled a ritual from a year before, when I had been working on a U.S. Forest Service helicopter crew in Idaho. Harold—our pilot—and I would climb into the ship, bound for some risky mission in the mountains. We'd conscientiously perform our respective preflight checks, then Harold would turn to me grinning and key the intercom. "Well," he'd drawl, "nothing holding us back now but common sense." I would sardonically chuckle and flash a thumbs-up.

·   ·   ·   ·   ·   ·   ·   ·   ·   ·   ·   ·   ·   ·   ·

We both knew that common sense never worked. I smiled at the recollection, and reminded myself to buy another jug of washer fluid before I left town. That, at least, was common sense.

At the bookstore I was gratified to see a poster on the front door that announced my presence, but as I stomped wet snow off my boots, the bookseller looked sheepish.

"I don't have any of your books," he said.

What? Give me a break!—the event had been arranged a month before. However, I wasn't actually shocked. It's a credit to my experience, I suppose, that I had a case of the damn things in the back of my truck.

"No problem," I lied, and trudged out to fetch books. I could picture Harold's grin, and realized I'd much rather be flying toward a wildfire in the Bitterroots than bothering about washer fluid in Bemidji.

Back in the store I sat for an hour-and-a-half—sold zero books. Three people entered the premises. It was, after all, a Thursday afternoon. As Kurt Vonnegut has written: "Hi Ho."

But then a crowd of four burst in, one laden with a tripod, video camera, and lights. The bookseller asked me if I would help out with a television commercial. Caught by surprise (and roused from a stupor), I agreed.

The director, a large and brassy middle-aged woman who seemed to be a friend of the bookseller, outlined the scenario. Bathed in the unforgiving glare of the camera lights, I would hand a book to one "actor"—a male—then pretend to sign a volume for an interested and grateful female.

I'll just say it: this woman was the stereotypical dumb blond. I'm sorry, that's how it is. She was vapid, giggly, and overdressed, and after we had run through the "scene" three times, she finally focused on my book and said, "This looks neat. I just started reading."

Her male colleague was nonplussed, and immediately asked the question that was on my lips.

"How old are you, Christie?"

. . . .

The Snow Lotus

"Twenty-five," she said brightly. "But I never paid attention in school." No shit.

By then I was alert and feeling violated, but the deed was done, so I graciously thanked the bookseller for having me (so to speak), and left with my full case of books. (Even though they were neat, Christie didn't buy one.) I thought: wipe that grin off your face, Harold.

The sleet had stopped, but the temperature was dropping, and I was aware that the wet highway would soon be turning icy. Nevertheless, I made good time, and I was only forty miles from home and the woodstove when I hit the patch of *black ice*.

Actually, the ice itself isn't black—it's clear as window glass. That's the problem. The ice is so fresh and transparent that all you see is the black asphalt beneath. Visually, there's no difference between dry pavement and the hard, slick rink—and no graceful transition, especially at 60 mph. (Yes, I'd grown cocky, almost desperate to be home.)

When my tires struck the black ice I immediately lost control. There was no time to effectively react. The Toyota swerved to the right and off the highway in a spray of bumper-blasted snow. The embankment was steep, and for an instant I was sure the truck was going to roll, but it spun in a ninety-degree arc and I hit the slope almost dead-on. I was momentarily relieved until I thought about boulders. The pickup was plowing through deep snow, the windshield plastered white, and I involuntarily scrunched up my back and buttocks, anticipating an impact that would tear away the front end and crush the crankcase. Then the truck abruptly stopped, its momentum sapped, and I heaved a trembling sigh of relief. No damage.

I shut off the engine and stepped out into calf-deep snow. It was obviously impossible to retrace my tire tracks up that embankment, but like a startled cat I was curious to see what had ambushed me. I climbed back to the highway to inspect the black ice. It was so slippery I could barely stand on it. Small wonder I was in the ditch.

. . . .

An Easy Winter   137

A car was approaching and I backed several yards off the road. As the vehicle drew abreast, the driver leaned over, rolled down his window, and shouted an offer of assistance. At that moment, a second car—apparently surprised by the benevolent move and unable to effectively brake—skidded into his trunk with a dense thump of folding metal and shattering plastic. The Good Samaritan's stricken face was framed in the window as his car was bashed several feet forward.

Luckily, it was a low-impact collision and neither driver was hurt, but here was black ice indeed, and I was mortified. I felt at least partially responsible for the accident—not unlike the hitchhiker in Idaho who had tried to blame himself for my mistake in the motorcycle mishap. As the Good Samaritan surveyed the damage to his car I blurted an apology. He shrugged, "Not your fault."

The other driver, a middle-aged woman, was pale with fear and visibly shaking, but she got out of her car saying, "I'm OK, I'm OK," and as the two of them exchanged names and phone numbers I went to work on her right front fender. It was pushed back against the tire, and I pried it out with my hands. I had her turn the wheel to make sure it was clear.

Since I hadn't decided what to do about my own predicament, I declined their offers of a lift and both drove off. I kicked some headlight and grill debris off the highway and faced my truck. I figured I'd best get out of sight for the time being, before some other kind passerby ended up paying for good intentions.

As I tramped back to the Toyota I spotted a way out. An unplowed trail or service road angled off to the right—downslope—and eventually swung back to the highway. My truck was actually sitting on the trail, and perhaps in the low gear of reverse I could make headway.

I rocked the truck a few times to get moving, careful not to spin the tires, and to my surprise I easily achieved enough momentum to wallow for a hundred yards to where the trail intersected the highway. But the final forty feet were

.   .   .   .

The Snow Lotus

uphill—that steep embankment—and I stalled. I understood that patience would be the key.

Fortunately, along with the case of books, I had a shovel and a five-gallon pail of wood ashes in the back. I dug away most of the snow in front of the rear wheels and sprinkled ashes on the icy mantle beneath. The traction bought me a few feet of progress up the embankment. I backed down to pack the ruts, then hopped out to widen them with the shovel and scatter more ashes—then forward a few feet higher, and so on. I estimated twenty minutes to surmount the last dozen yards, if I had enough ashes. I suspect that many people don't realize how strenuous a book tour can be.

On my third or fourth run at the slope, another passerby stopped, and this Good Samaritan had the right stuff: a three-quarter-ton 4WD pickup with a snowplow. It pulled onto the shoulder and a weatherbeaten man and his teenage son climbed out to assess the situation. *My* first thought was to engage that authoritative plow, but being the humble rescuee, I was reluctant to suggest it. After some ritual pleasantries, and another dose of ashes, the pair tried pushing me up the slope. Their muscle power helped, but the man quickly appreciated the obvious. Nodding at his truck he said, "Might as well plow this trail."

He did, and with one more broadcast of ash I drove onto the shoulder of the highway like a gentleman. My rescuers were about to drive off with a wave and a smile, but I shouted, "Wait!"

I rummaged in the back for one of my books, scribbled an appropriate message on the title page, and thrust it through the truck window at the baffled driver. I explained that I was an author "on tour." He stared at the book, face blank, then said, "Oh!" He grinned. "Thanks!" He looked bemused, as if I were a well-meaning child or a harmless drunk who'd just handed him a wad of Monopoly money. I quickly turned away to avoid further explanation. As I drove off and waved, he was still gazing at the book, his son leaning over to see—

.   .   .   .

probably trying to decipher my handwriting. Merry Christmas, folks; no good deed goes unpunished.

On December 23rd it reached plus forty-four degrees with sunshine, and a couple of bare spots appeared on the local ski trail. At that time of year it would've been far less unusual to see *minus* forty-four, and Speedy, the Township caretaker, was having a tough time establishing the local hockey rink. Over the past decade he and I have tallied hundreds of hours "making" ice, and we've learned that creating a decent skating surface is more complicated than just pouring water on the ground to freeze. The process revolves around texture and density, and ambient air temperature is critical. With such balmy daytime highs, the only option was to flood at night, and Speedy requested that I join him that evening to help lay another stratum of ice "under the lights."

We met at the Fire Hall after supper and warmed up Engine #2, a pumper/tanker with a thousand-gallon tank and a "quick dump" butterfly valve in the rear. At the rink, following Speedy's hand signals, I backed the formidable rig through a narrow gate and onto the ice sheet. When we reached the far end, Speedy opened the butterfly valve, and water gushed out in a solid stream, bursting into a wide fantail as it hit the ice. The temperature was hanging in the mid-twenties—ideal—and the warm water was sheened in mist as it slowly spread over the rink like a frosting of quicksilver, reflecting the lights. Speedy waved me ahead in short jogs until the truck was empty, then we returned to the Fire Hall to refill.

It takes three loads to cover the rink, and during our shuttles Speedy and I discussed the abnormally mild winter and the prospects for an early and sizzling spring. We're both seasonal wildland firefighters, and if April and May are dry there's money and adventure to be gleaned in northern Minnesota. We speculated about potential paychecks and traded tales of past glory. The stories were familiar, oft-repeated vignettes that either of us could've told, but we laughed as

.   .   .   .

cheerfully as we had the first time we heard them. It's not the content that counts, so much as the camaraderie of the telling and the hearing. Our fire stories are not information per se, but liturgy, and it makes us happy to share the rite.

And I needed a lift. For weeks I had cycled in and out of depression—the brand of background darkness that seems unlinked to everyday events. Several times I felt the pressure of tears for no obvious reason, and to be so down and blue without explicit cause is itself distressing, and initiates a vicious cycle of feeling bad about feeling bad. The background blackness is like dense, becalmed overcast, blocking the sunlight you're certain is beyond, but are powerless to reach. Perhaps most disturbing is the depression's neutrality and essential fairness. Just as bad events seem to play little role in its generation, good events have little effect on its dissipation. The bland impermeability of the overcast is what renders it so potent.

But occasionally, in a surge of hope materializing like a favorite song on the radio, some episode would have a winsome impact. I saw it as a break in the clouds, or as waves of radiation in my mind, rippling an ether that shaded from dark blue to glowing orange. Flooding the rink and talking about wildfire was an unexpected means to such light and clarity, and the elevated mood lasted for a couple of hours.

I sensed it fading around 10:00 P.M., and thus accelerated the downturn by simply acknowledging it. But a little after 11:00, as Pam and I were settling into bed, the phone rang. I hesitated, thinking to let the machine pick it up, then on impulse I grabbed it.

Without preamble I heard our friend Catherine launch into an enthusiastic description of Mars and Regulus. They were rising together just behind the gibbous moon. "The colors!" she said. "They're vivid!" I smiled. Yes, the colors— I could see my blue shifting slightly to orange, and the break in my mind's overcast that seemed to mirror Catherine's marveling account of the real sky. Her tone was infectious. I thanked her for calling and meant it more than she knew.

.   .   .   .

Then I gazed out the east-facing office window to admire the star and planet for myself.

Maybe it was the vibrant human connection, I thought, that could penetrate the darkness—Speedy and our bond of fire, Catherine and our shared passion for the sky. What a vigorous narcotic is human contact, the touching of minds, the melding of sensibilities. Shared work, a story, a fortuitously timed phone call—any of these may embody healing, no less welcome if it is only fleeting. After hall, transience is the core of an individual life.

Four days later, at sunrise, I heard a light patter on the roof. Rain? In late December? I rose from bed and peered out the west upstairs window. Yes, it was raining. How bizarre. Then I blinked in surprise and called to Pam, the custodian of my psyche and my ultimate human connection: "A rainbow!" Indeed, a perfect luminous arc.

It was something new to my sight to view such a phenomenon in the week joining Christmas and New Year's Day. I rushed downstairs, threw on a parka and stepped into my boots, then hurried out into the yard for a better look. I just made it. The sun must have been peeking through a rip in the overcast, because in less than a minute the rainbow abruptly vanished, as if someone had turned a switch.

Was it an omen? I was tempted to follow that thought, to promote my hopes and desires to some celestial cusp, then formulate a prophecy to be acted out or acted on. But I was unprepared.

I do not scorn the efficacy of omens. In modern terms they are "information" or "input." Webster says of *omen*: "a thing or happening supposed to foretell a future event." We could plug a financial statement from a stockbroker into that definition, or the score on an IQ test. But we don't, because those prophecies are glazed—for good or ill—with a patina of science and mathematics. Omens are *poetic* information, and that's why you'll often be favored with arched eyebrows if you talk about them too much or too seriously. Our culture relegates the poetic to a narrow slot in a mere

·   ·   ·   ·   ·   ·   ·   ·   ·   ·   ·   ·   ·

curriculum, labeling it *art*, pretending there is some defini-
tive gulf between art and life.

I say I was unprepared, because the most reliable omens
are those you are searching for. You cannot look out a window unless you know where it is, and omens are to routine
thought as plate glass is to the stained and leaded fenestellas
in the rampart of a cathedral. I had not urged myself: "Pre-
pare for an omen." So the rainbow was merely beautiful.

It did occur to me, though, that in light of my high-flown
wildfire talk with Speedy, I could employ the rainbow as a
colorful indication that the coming fire season would be
snappy and active, and hence lucrative. It raveled like so: In
the ninth chapter of Genesis, God tells Noah that a "token of
the covenant" between them would be a rainbow, and part of
the agreement stipulated there would never be another great
worldwide flood. (Good. Moisture on that scale would certainly put a negative spin on fire season.) Then, in a poetic
paraphrase of a passage in the Second Epistle of Peter, I noted
that James Baldwin wrote: "God gave Noah the rainbow
sign, No more water, the fire next time!" Voilà, the rare, late-
December rainbow was an omen for a dry and fiery spring.

That prophecy was all in fun, but on the morning of January 9th I wondered if I hadn't been more rigorously poetic
than I had intended.

I was working at my desk when the fire department pager
went off. After the nerve-tingling alarm tone the county dispatcher said:

"Attention, Town of French Fire Department and Hib-
bing DNR, we have a report of a fire. . . ." and she gave an address. Say what? To appreciate my initial surprise you must
understand that the DNR (Department of Natural Resources)
is paged only for a wildfire. This was January!—with a blanket of snow. A glance at the thermometer showed it was ten
degrees below zero, Fahrenheit. Was there some miscue at
Midway Dispatch? She continued:

"Caller says there is a leaf pile on fire and they can't put
it out. It's near buildings."

.   .   .   .

My surprise deepened to bewilderment—they couldn't extinguish a *leaf pile*? In January, at minus ten degrees? Besides, with a continuous snow cover how could the fire spread to endanger structures? My own alarm was tripped— the one inside my brain that has reacted to hundreds of emergencies: there was something askew here, some key information was missing.

I acknowledged the page via my handheld radio, then threw on my turnout gear—glad that it's so well insulated. I suspected nastiness. During the four-mile drive to the scene, I scrolled a picture of the address through my memory. It was at the end of a cul-de-sac on Big Sturgeon Lake, where a half-dozen residences—some year-round, some seasonal— share a hill hemmed in by spruce bog. I remembered lawns, garages, nice homes. It's like a slice of suburbia sprung out of the woods.

Neil, one of "my" firefighters, was there when I arrived, and he was grinning. I had already seen the expanding column of dirty gray smoke.

"It's a *pile* all right," he said.

I strode into the smoke, and like the December rainbow, here was another new thing.

The "pile" was practically a historical artifact. At the rim of a slope that dropped steeply into bog, the local residents had constructed the world's largest compost heap. During decades of lawn and garden work the families had collected leaves, conifer needles, grass clippings, weeds—and dumped them down the hill, along with tree stumps, scrap lumber, a fifty-five-gallon drum, and at least one joint of PVC pipe. This pile, though densely compacted by precipitation and decomposition, had grown to the proportions of a small house. There were literally *tons* of organic material in a mound of seasonal strata that was twenty feet thick. And it was on fire.

Just as I walked up, a smoldering pocket of heat burst into flame, threatening to consume a living balsam, then "ladder" up into the branches of a large white pine. I

.   .   .   .

The Snow Lotus

knocked down the flames with a shovel and surveyed the rest of the mess.

About a quarter of the mound was burning, and it resembled a peat fire—burrowing slowly into the damp pile in a hot, smoky smolder. It could burn for weeks, like some monstrous dottle of charred tobacco.

One of our engines arrived, along with a DNR rig, and we attacked the heat with hoselines and hand tools, digging/probing/tunneling. We eventually settled on a *peat nozzle* as the most effective tool. It's a heavy steel tube about three feet long that tapers slightly at the bore. We could forcefully shove it into the matted compost, and, supplied with a hundred and fifty pounds of water pressure, the nozzle worked like a saw blade and drill, ripping kerfs and cavities into the pungent mountain. We worked at it for about four hours. The temperature rose to a sweltering twelve above, and we laughed about the first "wildfire" of the new year. No one could recall the local DNR ever being paged out in January, and it was obvious that The Leaf Pile Fire was going to become a minor Side Lake legend.

Despite the comic aspects, however, it was a relatively expensive operation, and someone would have to get a bill. Besides, if the fire had burned during dry weather in spring or autumn, it could have easily spread into grass and brush and on to the homes. Whatever else it might be, that pile was also a significant storehouse of fuel.

The residents who reported the fire—and supplied us with coffee during the "battle"—held a delicate position. They knew how the fire started, but refused to directly implicate the neighbor who was apparently responsible. Then, about two hours after we arrived, the neighbor's wife walked over, surveyed the scene, and announced, "I *told* him not to dump the woodstove ashes here!"

So we knew. This weird fire was another result of the easy winter. If snow cover had been closer to normal depths, the discarded embers would not have retained enough heat to melt completely through to the combustible pile below,

. . . .

much less ignite it. But that wasn't my fault. I mailed the neighbor a bill for two hundred and fifty dollars.

The weather stayed mild, with only five more subzero days in January. On the 28th it reached thirty-two degrees, and I skied six miles in early afternoon on smooth, fast trails. An hour after sunset I hiked out to Hal's island in Big Sturgeon Lake, following a packed trail across the ice. I was toting a towel and a sixpack. Hal had lit his sauna, and I was anticipating the deep, organic solace we would achieve in the wake of a wintertime steambath, sipping good beer and nurturing desultory conversation.

I was early, and Hal and I settled in next to the wood-fired cookstove in his kitchen, awaiting Pat and Jerry, a couple from across the lake that we'd both known for many years, and who also appreciated the palliative power of Hal's sauna. They were due around 7:00 P.M., and a few minutes before the hour Hal and I were startled when the bell on his telephone and the alarm on my pager jangled at the same moment. As the dispatcher's voice boomed out of the pager, I quickly stepped outside so it wouldn't interfere with Hal's phone call.

The dispatcher said: "Attention, Town of French First Responders. A fifty-nine-year-old male has collapsed in front of 7708 Greenrock Road—has a history of heart." I was relieved for an instant that it was not a fire call, and I wouldn't have to respond, forsaking my sauna. Then I made the terrible connection just as Hal hung up the phone and shouted, "That was Pat! Jerry collapsed. She thinks it's a heart attack."

Greenrock Road is just across the bay separating the island from the mainland, and I rushed down to the lake to retrace my route across the ice. I had a clear picture of the scenario: Pat and Jerry would've parked their car just ahead of my truck at the end of the road, then started hiking down an unplowed driveway leading to a wooded peninsula where they'd cut across the bay at the narrowest passage.

.   .   .   .

Taking the dispatcher's message literally, I angled off Hal's main over-the-ice trail, and headed directly for the designated address. It took five or six minutes to get there, and assuming we would be engaged in CPR, I reviewed the procedure in my mind. It had been two and a half years since I had had a refresher course. I told myself: "OK, OK, you'll do fine, you'll do fine." But I had to resist a disturbing urge to slow down, fighting a natural reluctance to face the challenge of a life-and-death emergency, especially an incident involving an acquaintance. Who would know how long it required me to struggle through the snow? Hal, twenty-five years my senior, was far behind. I knew that our first responders were on the way, and how much easier and less stressful it would be for me if they arrived first and shouldered this grave responsibility. But I did not slow down. After so many years as fire chief, this temptation to avoid difficult duty was familiar, and I had the antidote: as soon as I felt the yen to slow down, I speeded up.

I could vividly imagine Jerry prostrate in the middle of Greenrock Road, in front of the house and garage at 7708, but when I arrived there, panting, I found I was wrong. The road was empty. I was confused—had the first responders and ambulance already come and gone? No way.

I rushed to the house and rapped on the door. An elderly woman answered, and I asked about Jerry. She somberly pointed down the unplowed driveway to the peninsula. Damn! I'd wasted precious time. By hurrying to respond, I'd missed what I soon realized Hal had learned from Pat's phone call—Jerry almost made it to the lakeshore before he collapsed, and this address was merely the source of Pat's call to 911.

I jogged several yards down the narrow track and stopped to yell for Pat. No answer. I ran further and spotted the glow of a flashlight. In a moment I was on the scene I'd dreaded. Jerry was on his back in the snow, in the subtly leaden posture of the unconscious that seems to merge them with the ground. Pat was hunched over doing chest compressions,

.   .   .   .

and Hal, who'd taken the more pertinent route over the ice to the landing, was administering mouth-to-mouth respiration. A man from the address back on the road was hovering alongside with the light.

"I'll take over, Pat," I said, and gently nudged her aside. I figured she'd already participated enough.

Adrenaline and training are a potent blend. Although I had never done compressions on a real person, it seemed almost natural, and I experienced no hesitation. I located the base of the sternum, laid my palm flat on the breastbone—two finger-widths up—locked my elbows and pushed down. Even under the stress of the situation my first thought was that the practice mannikins were certainly well designed, because the action felt the same. I did hear the cartilage crack, which obviously doesn't happen on Resusci Anne, but I was so reassured by the familiarity of the feeling that I only noted it with detached satisfaction. My instructors had told me to expect that noise.

As I write this, exactly four months later, I'm struck by how detached it sounds. But that was it—I felt suspended above the stream of time, self-controlled by powerful biochemicals and the indoctrination of the emergency services. The popular imagination expects panic and/or paralysis at such a scene, and of course that sometimes happens, but often people undergoing extreme trial are also imbued with an awful serenity.

My senses were acute, fully engaged. My hands were *there,* as if charged with electricity and linked to my awareness with pulsing silver cables. My pager sounded again, and the tones seemed as loud as howls. The dispatcher was calling for fire personnel. Our first responders had requested more help and our rescue sled. They had apparently reached the end of the road and seen that it was going to be a difficult haul from the lakeshore to the ambulance.

"He's gone, I know he's gone," said Pat, as Hal and I continued to work. I mentally filled in the unspoken details. When Jerry collapsed, Pat had to make a terrible choice: stay

. . . .

The Snow Lotus

with him and initiate CPR, or leave him to summon help. Wisely opting for the latter, she had to struggle back through the snow to the nearest occupied house, make the two phone calls (one to 911, the other to Hal for more immediate aid), then hurry back down the peninsula. This all required several long minutes, and Jerry had necessarily lain unattended.

"You did the right thing, Pat," I said, and meant it. If she had remained to perform CPR alone, she would have soon been exhausted and perhaps become a second victim. Even if she had managed to revive Jerry, she would've been unable to carry him to the road, and there was no guarantee he would not have relapsed anyway. Help was mandatory, and the more quickly it was summoned the better. It is a diamond-edged fact that due to inherent remoteness, a medical emergency in the backwoods is automatically more dangerous and complicated than it is in, say, a suburban shopping mall or a major airport terminal.

And I was also sure that Pat was right—Jerry was gone. Hal and I were ventilating and compressing a corpse. The pallor of Jerry's face lent it the sheen of stone, and the instant my hands touched his chest I did not expect to hear him cough or see his eyelids flutter. Nevertheless, once begun, CPR must continue until a declaration of death is made by someone officially qualified to do so, or until the rescuers are simply unable to go on.

With flashlights bobbing, four of our first responders approached out of darkness, including P. B., an EMT and Red Cross instructor with several years of experience on ambulance crews. She took charge.

Since Hal and I were already performing CPR, and our technique was satisfactory, P. B. and her crew set up the defibrillator, an electronic device that monitors heart rhythms and delivers an electric shock if necessary. When they were ready to attach the sensors/electrodes to Jerry's chest, Hal and I moved aside at the end of a compression cycle and first responders eased into our positions, without, as they say, missing a beat.

.   .   .   .

I stood up and backed off, holding high the flashlight one of the medics had given me. I was fascinated by P. B.'s hands. Though quick and sure as they manipulated wires and switches, I could plainly see them trembling. It was a stark incongruity with the level tone of her voice and the practiced efficiency of her actions. A casual bystander might have interpreted the trembling as nervousness or fear, but I knew better. Her hands were cold.

It wasn't as much due to the January night air—it was mild, in the high twenties, and she had worked hard to reach the scene—as it was due to her glandular secretion of epinephrine. I was watching a natural biochemical reaction to sudden stress. Among other things, blood leaves the extremities, making them colder and in need of slight shivering to maintain body temperature. P. B. was in the intense response mode—in some ways her natural habitat—but her hands trembled in mimicry of melodramatic terror, a reaction beyond her control and thoroughly out of tune with her calm, almost placid demeanor. Her hands were cold.

That small, seemingly trivial detail remains with me as one of the most vivid recollections of the night. It may be that I don't wish to recall with utter lucidity how Jerry's face looked against the snow that we all soon trampled to sugar (though I believe I do recall), but I think it transcends that. P. B.'s trembling hands were an avatar of life, a clear demonstration of both the resilience and frailty of the human entity, an affirmation of purpose and energy. They shook, yes, but those nimble hands were as vigorous as beating wings. Perhaps I focused on those fingers, on that movement, because I knew that Jerry was dead—unmoving and unmovable.

But the defibrillator indicated that it might not be so. Once it was up and monitoring, the machine, with a weird robotic rasp, uttered a startling command: "Stand clear," it said.

"It's going to deliver a shock," said P. B. "Stay clear, especially since we're all standing in snow." She didn't want any unintended "shockees."

. . . .

Jerry bucked and twitched as the current jolted his quiet heart. The defib had detected electrical activity in his chest and decided to administer a boost. The heart did not respond, and the medics resumed CPR.

By then two of our firefighters had arrived with the rescue sled. Six of us, three per side, knelt next to Jerry and lifted him into the sled—like pallbearers, I thought. I noticed his black galoshes, rubber overshoes with metal hooks and clasps instead of laces. They looked out of place in the backwoods, but close enough: Jerry had died with his boots on, and that suddenly seemed important.

But CPR was still in order, and as the two firefighters and I strained to drag the sled uphill, the first responders took turns performing compressions and breaths while on the move. Ahead, between the treetops, I saw the pulsating red glow of the ambulance beacons. It was only about a hundred and fifty yards, but it seemed like a journey. Perhaps I was impatient. Everyone was doing their duty—and well—but I couldn't suppress the feeling that it was time to leave Jerry alone. Let him go. But that was easy for me to think, and I really had no objective reason to believe that he might not make it. I was simply convinced that the internal girandole of vitality that we knew as Jerry had been extinguished, transcending the concerns of auricles, ventricles, and pulse.

Once we reached the plowed road and hefted Jerry through the ambulance doors, we were reduced to bystanders—helpless speculators of fate—though I soon learned that our EMS people shared my conviction that he was dead.

Hal intended to drive Pat to the hospital, and he asked me to hike back out to the island to make sure the stove was off, and to snuff out all but one of the kerosene lamps.

It was not an unpleasant walk. In contrast to the anxious rush across the ice less than an hour before, the soft snow—an obstacle then—was like a cushion. Strangely, I remembered that previous traverse as being *loud*. I suppose it was the echoes of the voice in my head, consciously fighting fear

.   .   .   .

and the temptation to delay. This walk was quiet, muffled by fatigue and the lowering overcast that was helping to keep us warm. I was grateful for that. I shuddered to think of our suffering if it had been minus thirty or forty degrees — cold hands indeed.

The stove was off, and I killed the kerosene lamps, gradually flooding the cabin with darkness except for a pool of yellow light in the kitchen. On the path to the ice, hemmed in by towering pines, I paused to look back at the dim glow in the kitchen window. It reminded me of the faint halo of the Andromeda galaxy as seen in the lenses of my binoculars, or of a distant campfire screened by trees and evening mist. That, I thought, is a portrait of ephemeral human life in the universe.

During the second week in February I helped to teach a basic wildland firefighting course for the DNR, and anticipation permeated the atmosphere. The wishful thinking about a long fire season that Speedy and I had indulged while flooding the rink in December was proving prophetic. The winter continued to be anemic, and even in February we already appeared to be entering the season I call "sprinter" — the hermaphroditic combo of late winter and proto-spring that feeds off its own oscillations between teasing warmth and vindictive resurgences of cold. Sprinter usually strikes in mid-March, but from February 22nd through 24th, for example, I recognized some unmistakable signs: under clear night skies the temperature hung at thirty degrees; our nearest neighbor spotted a skunk in our driveway; the ski trails were glazed, a product of the mercurial swing from forty-four degrees above on the 22nd to one below on the morning of the 24th. The winter was dying young, and it is not insignificant that on February 21st, Hal and I took a CPR refresher course taught by P. B. We were attentive students.

On March 4th I heard a news report about a couple in a nearby town who had been asphyxiated in the night by car-

.   .   .   .

The Snow Lotus

bon monoxide from a malfunctioning heating system. A dog was also dead, and a child was in the hospital. Tragic.

On March 5th, I unfolded the first section of the Sunday newspaper and discovered with a shock that the male victim was Danny, an old friend and coworker, age forty-two. We had spent five years together at the sewage treatment plant, and he was still employed there.

The next day I drove into town to commiserate with my erstwhile colleagues at the plant. As soon as I opened the door I experienced an intense flashback. It was the smell— not entirely unpalatable, but strong, especially to a nose that was no longer acclimated to the powerful olfactory cues of a sewage treatment operation. The odor temporarily obliterated the past decade, and I could have been walking on shift, ready for duty. It was disturbing, particularly in light of my purpose. I too could have worked there until I died.

Jimmy and Tom were in the control room, and they told me that the previous Friday, only several hours before his death, Danny participated in a discussion about wakes, and how he would like his to be conducted. A week earlier he had quit smoking, remarking that it was something he wanted to accomplish before he died. Premonitions? Certainly. Mere coincidences? Certainly. Take your pick.

After a half-hour of chitchat and reminiscing, I left, knowing the once familiar odor would cling to my clothes like the sadness I felt for Danny. But I was also relieved that I had not worked at the plant for a single second in the last ten years. Leaving that job had cost me about $100,000 in missed wages (not to mention the worth of forsaken benefits), but it was a bargain. Nevertheless, the events of the next day might not convince an impartial observer.

Back in February the *New York Times Book Review* had run a prominent and favorable review of my book *Hellroaring,* thus generating some collateral publicity. It seemed in keeping with the oddity of the winter. The publishers even had a couple of nibbles from film people, and I wasn't sure if I should rejoice, or apply for an unlisted phone number and a

·   ·   ·   ·   ·   ·   ·   ·   ·   ·   ·   ·   ·

new identity. No movie deals actually surfaced, but National Public Radio's "Fresh Air" program did arrange an interview, and on March 7th I drove to a Minnesota Public Radio station in Duluth to be electronically linked to the "Fresh Air" folks in Philadelphia. I had been assured by friends in the radio business that this was a big deal—on a par with the *New York Times* itself. I decided to believe it, and arrived in Duluth feeling slightly exalted. This would probably be more stimulating than performing in a bookstore commercial in Bemidji.

There had been a heavy snowfall in Duluth the day before—a storm we'd happily missed in Side Lake—so I allowed extra time for navigation and parking, and arrived at the station about a half hour early. To pass the time I browsed in a nearby Waldenbooks store. My exalted mood was humbled. Though I had five books in print—two of which had been blessed with favorable reviews in the *New York Times*—not a single damn copy of any of my titles was stocked in the store. Not one. I hadn't considered it unreasonable to expect that the two latest volumes—released only several months before—would at least be represented by a few units. I would have introduced myself to the manager and offered to autograph them. After all, I was essentially a local author. Perhaps they had recently sold out. Yeah, right. The cold truth was apparent: I was going to do an author interview on a national broadcast network at a microphone a stone's throw from a national chain bookstore (a hundred miles from my home) that wasn't carrying my books.

When I left the store I was probably just subdued enough to be properly relaxed for the interview—slightly to the right edge of "Who gives a damn?"

Four days later, genuine spring arrived like an earthquake. In his seven decades, Hal could not recall a faster meltdown, and I certainly couldn't. It began on the 10th with an afternoon high of forty-six degrees, and for the next five days we enjoyed daytime temperatures in the fifties and

.   .   .   .

overnight lows above freezing. On the 13th the coolest it got was the mid-forties. (Felt like June, as I heard someone quip.) Squirrels were mating in the mud. Our easy winter was clearly finished.

On the 11th, a halcyon day that had seen fifty-six degrees and sunshine, Hal invited five of us out to the island for a sauna—the first time he'd lit the stove since the night of Jerry's death. Pam fixed up a cauldron of chili, and as that simmered in the kitchen, we lounged in the glow of the livingroom hearth, sipping beer and wine. It was an articulate, engaging group, and I let the conversation wrap around me like a down comforter, saying little. It was simply a pleasure to hear my friends.

I volunteered to stoke the sauna and check its progress, and after a couple of trips to the firebox I announced that it was prime. The temperature at the top bench was around 180 degrees. We gathered up our towels and fresh clothes and trooped in single file down the narrow ridgetop path from the cabin to the sauna.

Catherine was behind me and she said, "Is something wrong?"

"No, why?"

"You're so quiet."

I smiled over my shoulder. "Just listening."

It was the best thing to do—reveling in the silence of snow and stars, eavesdropping on the death throes of an easy winter.

.   .   .   .

⑨ Smoking Mountain

.
.
.
.
.
.
.
.
.
.
.

Ice is the silent language of the peak. . . .
CONRAD AIKEN

When I came to I saw that Brute was still out cold, lying on his back in the volcanic ash. We were fortunate that this wasn't some hairy technical climb, where we were inching around rock outcrops or depending on handholds, because it was the second time in a half hour that we had both passed out. Our elevation was about 16,000 feet, and the air was lean.

I slipped my battered Pentax Spotmatic out of the camera bag, and bracing against the slope, squeezed off a shot of the prostrate Brute. His pals would be amused. He had earned his nickname via convincing displays of machismo, and no one had seen him like this—unconscious and helpless—unless it was the guy who had awarded Brute the busted-up, misshapen nose that fit his face so well.

I tucked the Pentax away and dug my boots into the ash. It was like black, granular snow, ankle deep, and nasty to trudge through. But at least when we lost consciousness and dropped, the cushioned impact gouged a depression and we didn't roll away. I stood up, craned my neck, and surveyed the top of Popocatepetl. We were near the edge of the snow-pack, a dazzling canescence against the violet-blue of the alpine sky. Only via jetliner had I ever penetrated higher into the atmosphere, and I understood that we should have packed some oxygen bottles. Popo peaks out at 17,930 feet, and we were determined to shout from the summit.

The driver we had hired that morning in Mexico City had delivered Brute and me and four of our companions to around the 12,000-foot level, and from there the ascent seemed straightforward—a one-mile hike. It was steeply up-slope, to be sure, but less than 6,000 feet. Brute and I were serious distance runners, and I had just completed my fourth marathon only two months before. How tough could this walk be?

But our aerobic vigor had been established in East Texas, in the rich, moist breezes a few hundred feet above sea level, and after several minutes of slogging skyward through the ash, I was gasping for each breath, temples drumming—gradually drowning in open air.

After an hour of toil, Brute and I were alone at about 15,000 feet, the others having fallen back. They were mere specks far below, and Brute chided them in absentia for their lack of fitness and resolve. I self-righteously clucked in agreement, and shortly thereafter we fainted for the first time.

That scared us a little, but we were colts—budding, strong, and overwhelmed by the surreal vistas that we earned with each step. A single glance encompassed a range of ecosystems that pitched up from a verdant patchwork of farms and tropical fruit trees in the distant valley, through foothills thick with conifers, to the lunar landscape of ash, swallowed eventually by glittering snowpack—all vaulted by the manifest dome of *el cielo*.

After photographing Brute, I waited for him to open his eyes. He sat up and squinted at me.

"Race you to the top," I said.

He grunted at the unlikely notion and hooked a thumb downslope. "Well," he grumbled, "at least we've made it higher than those pups."

We resumed our tortured hike, and I noticed that the neighboring peak, Iztaccithuatl, only 600 feet lower than Popo, and forming the opposite rampart of the valley, was now wreathed in dense cloud that seemed to be cascading down its flanks like the billowing froth of a cataract. A few minutes later the first wisps of cloud appeared directly overhead, and our goal was partially obscured.

We reached the boundary of the continuous snow cover, discovering it was only lightly crusted and couldn't reliably support our weight. Every two or three steps we broke through, knee deep. I dragged in a huge breath and rasped, "The ash was better."

A few moments later—I guess—my eyes fluttered open and I felt the snow sucking heat out of my back. Brute was standing a little way upslope, waiting. Luckily, he didn't have a camera. It was too much effort to talk anymore, and we silently pushed on to about 17,000 feet, lungs afire. By then we were in the midst of cloud, and suddenly the air was saturated with wind-driven snowflakes and visibility dropped to a few yards. My sweat was cold and I shivered. We crouched in the snow and stared at each other. We had achieved a plane of intensity where words were superfluous. This perilous moment was as near and present as our skin.

Brute shook his head. I nodded. We staggered to our feet and half-walked, half-slid down to the ash, then followed our boot prints back into the sunlight at 12,000 feet.

We laughed at our naïveté, chastened and contrite, realiz-

.   .   .   .

ing that Popocatepetl had probably been kind to a pair of overconfident *gringos* who thought to skip to the top for lunch. We had blithely proceeded under the spell of those fraternal twins, arrogance and ignorance. We were dulled by our youthful pride, and by a single-minded trust in beauty. Arrogance and ignorance are always deceivers, and beauty is sometimes merely a warning, or perhaps bait for the unmindful. In his autobiography, *Naturalist*, researcher and theorist E. O. Wilson discusses certain species of brightly colored ants, whose cosmetics probably serve to alert would-be predators to their formidable stingers or highly toxic secretions. "In the natural world," Wilson writes, "beautiful usually means deadly. Beautiful plus a casual demeanor *always* means deadly."

And what was more casual and benign than Popocatepetl viewed from a distance—a silent snowcap sparkling in the sun, haloed by heavenly blue? And in our swagger we called her "Popo," an inattentive liberty that disregarded the meaning of her full Aztec name: Smoking Mountain. Only years later did I learn that Popocatepetl is an *active* volcano. The last major eruption was in 1702, but as recently as 1943 there was an explosion of ash—perhaps what Brute and I had hiked through—and it's not uncommon for clouds of gas and smoke, and sometimes rock, to pour from the crater. (As I write this, in December 1994, a major eruption seems imminent and nearby towns are being evacuated.)

Would this knowledge have stopped us? Probably not, but it may have inspired a level of respect and preparation that would have helped us attain the summit.

Two days later we were riding the rails from Mexico City to the Texas border at Nuevo Laredo, sharing a train with peasants, goats, and machine-gun–toting *Federales*. It was a twenty-four-hour run, and at dusk I balanced on a small platform between cars, watching a limpid twilight over shimmering desert in San Luis Potosi. The bittersweet euphoria of travel washed over me—a maudlin blend of home-longing and genuine affection for an exotic locale already receding into memory. Besides Popocatepetl, we had also scaled the Pyramid of the Sun, standing quietly at the apex as storm clouds crested the surrounding ridges and hair rose on the back of our necks. My Pentax recorded a particularly gory bullfight, and most of us suffered roaring assaults of Montezuma's revenge. We had wagered on *jai alai* and attended the Ballet Folklórico. It had been a tourists' slice-of-Mexico journey, filled with noise and color, and as we rocked north through the desert I assumed the best was over.

But next morning we pulled into a squalid little village that seemed to have sprung from the arid dirt itself. Anemic fields surrounded a ramshackle collection of adobe huts, and the citizens looked as gaunt and weathered as the land—or so it seemed to a young North American with boundless prospects and a wad of dollars.

The train stopped for about ten minutes, and I stepped out between the cars to get a better look at the town. I was instantly besieged by seven or eight small boys, perhaps five to ten years old. They reached up from the ground, palms open, begging for money. I had a pocketful of Mexican coins that would do me scant good across the border, so I fished them out. Without thinking, I shoved the pesos into one of the little hands, and all hell broke loose. The lucky kid grabbed the coins, lunged out of the knot of his fellows, and sprinted away. With an angry shout the others tore after him, and I groaned. How stupid could I be? Why hadn't I been considerate enough to dole out the coins, making sure everybody got at least one? I feared that those kids I had thoughtlessly spurned were going to catch the "lucky" one, rough him up, and take the money—then perhaps fight among themselves. I certainly hadn't contributed to their sense of comradeship.

The boy got about thirty yards before they snagged him, and I watched—anxious and embarrassed—from the platform, waiting for the ugliness to commence. But it didn't. To my surprise and delight (and relief) they merely led him, unstruggling, back to me. Pushing him forth like a defen-

. . . .

dant in front of a judge, they pointed and waved, rattling away in Spanish. I caught the drift. They wanted me to tell him to share the loot. I spread my hands to indicate the group, and trying to appear both kind and stern, I looked him in the eye and said, "Sí, sí . . . a su amigos, el dinero a su amigos, por favor."

He wasn't thrilled, but he did it, grudgingly placing a coin into the outstretched hands of his beaming companions. I was glad, but also ashamed at having assumed that they would take the money by force. It was now clear that because I had given the coins to the one boy, they were his—as unfair as it was. His pals would not take their "share" without my leave. These panhandling children kept a code of honor, and I wondered if I would have done the same at their age, acted with such a sense of respect—not only for their opportunistic friend, but also for a bungling adult who caused unnecessary trouble.

This, I realized—red-faced—was the kind of deference Brute and I should have offered to Popocatepetl. It is always best to assume and ascribe dignity and potency, no matter what the outward appearance. The world runs on courtesy, whether it's the transfer of pesos, or the scaling of a snow-capped peak.

As the train started to move I waved to the boys, and the "lucky" one raised an arm and pointed at his wrist. "Su reloj!" he shouted. "Su reloj, por favor!"

I laughed. He wanted my watch!

I almost threw it to him. After all, he did say "please."

⑨ Farewells

.
.
.
.
.
.
.
.
.
.

By a knight of ghosts and shadows
I summoned am to tourney.
from TOM O' BEDLAM, Anonymous

Three years in a row I left home for the summer. I had a job
with the U.S. Forest Service in Idaho, battling wildfires. My
specific position was in "helitack," as a member of a helicopter crew. Our missions included initial attack on fires,
medevacs, search and rescue, reconnaissance (visual and
infrared), slinging cargo, and the support and retrieval of
smokejumpers. It's considered dangerous work, and we
earned a lot of "H-pay," that is, a "hazard differential" akin
to military combat pay. It was 25 percent of our base rate
per hour, and was coveted almost as much as overtime.

Though I had a decade of fire experience when I arrived in Idaho, I was nervous . . . no, scared. Fireground aviation was a different league, a ratcheting up of the stakes. Only a few years before, one of my predecessors on the crew had been decapitated by a tail rotor. He made *one* mistake that triggered a quick chain reaction of unstoppable events. In less than five seconds a helicopter was destroyed, a pilot was injured, and the helitack crew member was dead.

On the day before I left for Idaho that first year, I walked down to Secret Lake at dusk and stood on the dock. In a spontaneous gesture of farewell I spread my arms as if to hug a friend, and held that position for several minutes. I listened to the ripples, inhaled the perfume of the bog, surveyed the forest horizon of birch, spruce, and pine. I took a mental time exposure, imprinting the milieu and attempting to freshly experience the familiar setting as if I had never been there. But I also conjured the memories of so many sweet and revelatory moments spent on Secret Lake. Our cabin is comfortable and soothing, but when I think of "home," I picture that spot on the rim of the bog. It's a portal to the numinous, a haven for the spirit. At sundown, sunrise, or midnight, the lake is a looking glass, a wonderland where soul and water mingle with light.

As I stood with my arms in the air, I realized it was possible I was there for the last time, that I might not return from Idaho. It wasn't *likely* I would be killed, but given the nature of the work, it was certainly possible. A lump rose in my throat. Never be *here* again? My perception intensified at the thought. I beckoned the impressions, consciously willing my sight to be keen, my hearing acute—burning that twilight moment into my brain. I felt my arms rise higher, and was suddenly electrified, tingling briefly with sheer, innocent affection for everything. I used to call that prayer.

Next morning I embraced Pam amid tears, promising to be home before the leaves fell from the trees. I did not tell her of my farewell to Secret Lake, but during the 1,400-mile drive I thought a great deal about them both, and when I arrived at my duty station in Idaho I felt compelled to pen a farewell letter, just in case.

It was strange and difficult to write from the perspective of a ghost, knowing the words would be read in anguish. What tone to take? Surely it was possible to be too light-hearted, yet there was no point in waxing lugubrious. About halfway through I almost gave up, suddenly remembering the one letter *I* had received from the dead.

Back in 1975 my close friend John Niemi had ventured on a moose hunting trip to Manitoba. He wrote me shortly after he arrived, and a couple days later he was accidentally shot to death by one of his companions. I received the letter just after his funeral, and clearly recall the wave of shock and desolation when I pulled the envelope from our mailbox and recognized the handwriting. I was so upset, I tossed it into the woodstove.

But, I reasoned, John's had not been written as a farewell letter, and was therefore only depressing. Mine would be a purposeful attempt to help assuage grief. It probably wouldn't work well at first, but might be treasured later, as gloom and shock abated. Besides, I was a writer, so what the hell—had to squeeze in a final essay no matter what.

After a couple of painful drafts I was finally satisfied, and slipped the work into a stamped envelope addressed to Pam. I sealed that envelope into a larger one and boldly wrote on the outside: TO BE OPENED IN THE EVENT OF MY DEATH.

Each of the thirty or so firefighters that worked at the base was assigned a mailbox (an open slot, actually) in the ready room, and I placed my letter—face down—at the bottom of my slot. I was uneasy about it. I wasn't sure how my colleagues would react if they knew I was preoccupied enough with the possibility of death to write a farewell letter to my spouse. It might not be good for morale; I might be regarded as too fatalistic, and hence unprofessional; I might just be considered weird. I made sure no one was in the room when I slipped the letter into the box.

But over the next few weeks I noticed that mine was not

.   .   .   .

the only envelope that never budged. We spent a lot of time in the ready room with the boxes in plain view, and it was simple to note that some of the same "mail" was always there at the bottom of various slots. Could it be that I was not the only ghost?

I was consumed by curiosity, and one day—guilt-ridden about tampering with mail, but unable to quell the lust of my suspicion—I sidled up to the boxes when no one was around and quickly pulled a conspicuous bottom-dwelling envelope from a slot near mine. I turned it over and read: TO BE OPENED IF I KICK. I stuffed it back in—face down—and strode away grinning. I knew that guy well; how appropriate that the young buck could apparently not bring himself to write the word "death." But that was OK, we were on the same wavelength, and I would rather work with firefighters who acknowledge their mortality than with those who believe they're indestructible.

So I established a tradition, and the following two years it was thus: on the evening before I left home I prayed on the shore of Secret Lake, and when I arrived at the base I wrote that damn letter. And each September, at the end of the season, I was pleased to tear up those envelopes and sprinkle the small pieces into a wastebasket. Then, two days later and 1,400 miles farther east, I would present my arms to the lake and say, "I'm home."

Byron wrote: "All farewells should be sudden."

And they are—past us in moments, as life itself. But one way to make a moment endure, to preserve the fruit and farewell of a fleeting dusk, is to gaze through the eyes of a ghost.

·   ·   ·   ·   ·   ·   ·   ·   ·   ·   ·   ·   ·

The Snow Lotus

PETER M. LESCHAK is a freelance writer who lives in northeastern Minnesota. His books include *Letters from Side Lake,* published in paperback by the University of Minnesota Press (1992), *The Bear Guardian* (1990), which won a Minnesota Book Award, and *Seeing the Raven,* published by the University of Minnesota Press in 1994. He is also a freelance wildland firefighter, and works fires across the United States for various state and federal agencies.